Team

Applying lessons from neuroscience to improve
Collaboration, Innovation and Results

LORI SHOOK &
FRODE SVENSEN

Table of Contents

Notes from the Authors

Frode Svensen

It feels a bit weird to admit that you start a company and write a book because you are frustrated, but that is the truth.

I have worked in the field of developing people for most of my thirty-year long career, as a supervisor, manager and consultant. I have delivered great training programmes for people coming from all parts of an organisation. At the end of these programmes, the leaders would be fired up and ready to go home and implement their learning. I met many of them a year or two after their programme, and over and over I heard the same: "People back at the office weren't as receptive as the folks at the course; it was hard to get my people on board; I felt weird trying these new skills; the skills didn't seem to work with my people. They all seem to duck and say to themselves: yeah, yeah, let's just let the boss get back to normal. It usually takes a couple of weeks after he's been to a leadership course."

I felt bad for them, and I grew more and more frustrated by the work we did: Great training and lots of learning, but little implementation.

Why is that? Is it true that what we taught on the course does not work in the real world? Or is it true that we have given these participants a Mission Impossible:

Go back to work and implement the skills you have just learned. However, your people back at the office do not know what you are trying to accomplish. You have learned nothing about how to train your team to respond to your new approach. Nor have you learned that at first it will be normal that they will resist the changes you have made. In addition, you are on your own, because there is no support to help you to implement these new skills.

Our company, shooksvensen, and this book are an attempt at improving the way we do culture change: We need to train people together, as a team, and give them lots of support in implementing the new skills back at the office. In addition, they need to realise that change takes time and that it helps to understand how the brain really works, especially when facing change.

Lori Shook

I am passionate about training. It is extremely satisfying to design and deliver engaging experiential programmes where learners leave inspired and can immediately practise their new behaviours in their real environments. Deeper learning will come for them with time and practice, of course, but I like to know that when those learners leave a course room, they have everything they need – including the motivation – to start using their newly acquired skills.

It is natural for people to enjoy learning and even have fun with it. Unfortunately, most of our current teaching models would not be described as enjoyable nor fun. It is time to be done with those approaches. There is quite a movement in education. I say, let us make such a movement in corporate learning situations as well.

People are more open to learning when they are having a good time. They are more willing to try something new when the atmosphere is light and non-judgemental. We must create a positive environment and invite them to try out the things we want them to learn. They need to learn how to do it, not just think about how it could be done.

I have had the good fortune to learn the essentials of experiential learning when I delivered programmes for an organisation that was known for their engaging training courses. Over fifteen years of experimenting with different styles of delivery and paying attention to what people actually retained from those programmes, I developed some of my own personal theories about what really creates learning. It was exciting to discover from my studies in neuroscience that many of my musings are real and can be explained by the science of the brain.

It is fairly straightforward how we learn and retain capabilities. We can use that knowledge to design brain-friendly programmes, to deliver engaging programmes and to effectively follow up with people to support them in the real learning, which takes place over time.

Acknowledgements

A lot of people have helped us write this book; some of them probably do not even know it. First, we would like to thank all the people we have trained and coached over the years. They have given us the material we needed to create the Sekhmed team and much of the knowledge we have about what works and what doesn't work in the field of Leadership Development and Culture Change.

Another big thank you goes to all the colleagues and friends we have worked with over the years. In every training programme, workshop and team coaching session, we have learned something from you. We have shamelessly used all of that learning in this book.

We are very grateful to Sonia Duggan who is a fabulous storywriter. Thank you for turning our long and boring notes into a story that brings our characters to life. And thanks for all of your editing and help with anglicising the text.

Thank you to both Adrian Pancucci and Dorothy Atcheson for editorial help and comments made very early in this journey. Your participation and input was hugely valuable.

Thank you to Michael Southgate and Gwen Knowles. Your graphical assistance and mock up of our book cover was amazing. We tried and tried to create something we liked and then boom, you came out with a few magical solutions in no time at all.

Of course, a big thank you to Rob Kosberg who guided, gently prodded and helped us keep this project alive and to Rob's team for all of their editing and production work.

Daniel Doherty, thanks for your enthusiasm about our work.

John Izzo, thanks for your encouragement and for really getting what we are doing.

Thank you to the professionals in the field of neuroscience. Your research makes it possible for us to understand how the brain works, and you help us take the "soft" out of "soft skills." This has done so much to make our work more acceptable to a wider audience.

The work we do is clearly impacted by Marita Fridjhon and Faith Fuller who created CRR Global and Organisation and Relationship Systems Coaching (ORSC™). CRR Global is where we learned about systems thinking, systems coaching, and a systems approach to any work with organisations. Thank you, thank you.

Foreword

By John Izzo, PhD

Why did human beings become the dominant species on planet Earth? And why does that even matter? Be careful, because it is actually a trick question.

Your immediate response will probably be because we were smart and clever, which we most certainly are. But we were not the only clever species that has evolved on Earth. Whales actually have larger brain-to-body mass ratios than we do. Apes, gorillas and chimpanzees are also clever; they even use tools.

Our sight not so special, our sense of smell pretty poor, our strength not so mighty, our hearing middle of the pack, our offspring awfully dependent... on down the list we go until we come to the compelling reason we find ourselves, for the better or worse for the rest of the species, dominating the globe. The reason is simple: more than any other species, we learned to cooperate beyond our immediate families and even our tribes, and also because we kept consciously adapting. We are who we are because, in one form or another, we learned to work as a team.

Charles Darwin is famously known for the common myth about evolution which is "Survival of the fittest," as well as for writing: "In the long history of humankind (and animal kind too), those who learned to collaborate and improvise most effectively prevailed." Apes, whales, elephants and many other species demonstrate cooperation but usually only in small kinship-related groups. It may be that we should be named "homo cooperatus."

While it is true that individual effort and even competition drives survival, we became a super species because we harnessed the power of cooperation first to hunt, then to farm, and now to create a world wide web that connects an entire planet with the wisdom and knowledge of billions of people.

But of course anyone who has worked in an organization, been to school, or watched the evening news knows that while we succeeded because we are cooperative, we often foster a climate where people compete rather than collaborate.

Companies and organizations have awakened to the importance of teamwork and collaboration. Over the last two decades, I have consulted with over 500 organizations, and almost all of them tell me they want more teamwork, less silo thinking, more working across lines and disciplines. Yet individualism and a focus on my success, my part of the puzzle, my role and department continue to plague organizations. In fact, a senior associate at one of the largest employee survey providers in the world told me that when they ask workers all over the world "What one thing would make this company more successful?" the most written in word is – you guessed it – collaboration.

This book brings some fresh and compelling insight into how to develop true teamwork by taking us behind the scenes of the human brain, especially our "social" brain. By helping us see why we both need and desire to be part of a "tribe" and what causes us to act in opposition to true teamwork, the authors show us ways we can harness this knowledge both for ourselves and as leaders. The emerging study of neuroscience is changing our understanding of why we do what we do every day and also how to develop ourselves.

One of the most empowering things we are learning from this new research is that old dogs can learn new tricks. Our brains and capacity to learn are far more plastic that we ever imagined. On the one hand we get hard wired into habits because, as the authors point out, habits are very efficient. Yet they challenge us not to accept our natural reactions as destiny but to grow personally so that we can grow our teams.

For many years I told people that I don't really believe in organizational change. What I mean by that is that organizations don't change, people change. When enough people change, then, and only then, does the organization make a shift.

This books challenges us to harness the power of neuroscience to develop ourselves so that we can both lead teams and be great team members. It shows how organizations and leaders can drive personal development. By taking us through the story of one company, they help us connect the dots to a path forward.

The application of neuroscience to business and organizations is one of the most important leaps of our day. This book makes a meaningful contribution to how to apply it while showing how we can grow personally and collectively.

One human being alone is perhaps not a human being at all. We have always been a species that needed and chose to cooperate. Developing our capacity to do so more deeply and consistently will not only help organizations but will build the future we all want.

John Izzo, Ph.D is an international business consultant, keynote speaker and author. He has consulted for over 500 companies around the world and has written six bestselling books including Awakening Corporate Soul, Values Shift and Stepping Up. He can be reached at www.drjohnizzo.com

Introduction

Teaming Up

Western cultures tend to be individualistic in nature. We teach our children to be independent and self-empowered. We are expected to perform well as individuals – at school, at work and perhaps even in our families. We are raised to do our schoolwork as individuals, we are graded individually and the education system is, in many ways, inherently competitive: grades are often given on a scale that ranks students relative to their classmates. Therefore, a student needs to outperform fellow students in order to be deemed successful.

From a young age, we are asked, "What do you want to be when you grow up?" We search for our own personal values. We ask ourselves: *Who am I? How can I contribute? What are my skills and my strengths?*

After twenty years of being trained as independent thinkers in school and with our attention mostly focused on our individual success, our next goal is to land a plum job in a great company. Our salary, opportunities to work on the best projects, bonuses and promotions are all largely based on our individual achievements and performance. And then we are expected to work effectively on a team.

Team? How am I supposed to behave on a team? What does it even mean to be part of a team? Do I need to do better than everyone else on that team to get a better salary or bonus this year? Everything in my life experience screams: "Yes!" So how do I learn to be a team player? My salary is based on me as an individual, my accomplishments are mine as an individual, and I've been trained my whole life to thrive as an individual, so what do you mean, "team"?

Without consciously thinking about it, those of us brought up in an individualistic world probably won't even ask those questions. Instead we step into roles we've always known: take care of myself, do what's good for me, and compete with the others so I can be the best.

So much has been written about the need for effective teamwork, and companies around the world know they need to do so much more to harness the potential of their teams. Pretty much everything we do at work takes places in some kind of team. But it's not really working. Despite the great work done by many coaches, change management experts and team development consultants, silo thinking, blame and defensiveness, team dysfunction and internal competition all remain hale and hearty in organisations today. And given that most of us have been trained our whole lives to be independent and competitive, maybe the question should be: *Why are we so surprised by the problems?*

Some Helpful Lessons

We have learned many lessons from the recent explosion of work in neuroscience. One of these lessons is that in an effort to be efficient, the brain is quite good at creating habits – unconscious habits – so that we don't have to spend time thinking consciously every minute about how to behave. It just happens. We see that individualistic behaviour is just a long-held habit that has been strongly reinforced.

Lesson: the brain creates habits and relies on habits to function every day

Fortunately, neuroscience has also told us about "plasticity": our brains are not hardwired but are always changing, even into late adulthood. So we can still change! Even if we've been individualistic our whole lives, there's still a chance to learn how to team up and be more team focused. We just need to learn how.

Lesson: our brains are not hardwired – we can learn to do things differently.

It is a choice to be a team player. First we need to learn how and then we need to practise. Learning how to team up and encouraging companies to enhance teamwork is one of the main objectives of this book. We also wish to address some of the dysfunctions in organisations that occur when teams aren't functioning well.

Fear-based Brains

In the neuroscience chapter of this book, we describe the brain's focus on survival. In order to survive, there are needs to be met and threats to be avoided. This creates impulses to go for opportunities that seem to serve us personally and to avoid situations that might harm us. The result is a focus on personal gain and a strong tendency for fear-based reactions. The good news and bad news is that the definition of what might serve or harm is based largely on perception, experience and assumptions, so it is changeable and trainable.

> *Lesson: The brain's focus on survival drives us to be protective of our needs and fearful of perceived threats.*

From both systems thinking and neuroscience, we learn about our social behaviour. We are social animals; the brain is attuned to others around us and is always responding in relation to others.

> *Lesson: The brain is a social brain, designed to be in relationship with others.*

By combining our social nature and the brain's survival focus and fear reactions, it's easy to see that bringing people together in groups can be a recipe for disaster and dysfunction. Problems occur quickly, especially if people believe they are not safe and secure.

Many of the challenges in organisations stem from our survival-based needs and fears. Some of those needs include belonging, power, independence and control. Our innate fears include fear of failing, of not being good enough, of the unknown and of not being appreciated by others.

You'll notice that those needs and fears are all individual concerns, but they can only exist in relation to other individuals. They are individual and they are interpersonal. Multiply all those interpersonal needs and fears by the number of people in an organisation, and it's no surprise that there's a snarly mess of entangled, complicated, political relationships.

It's common to witness infighting, competition and individuals needing to out-perform their colleagues and to be seen and acknowledged emotionally and financially. Silo working and an "us versus them" culture gets created. Leaders are frustrated in their attempts to control the rank and file, because people just won't do what they're told to do. Assumptions lead to endless misunderstandings that lead to conflicts. But we're mostly conflict avoidant, so we bury the problems and are unaware that they show up in behaviour such as cutting sarcasm during a meeting, which then sets off a firestorm of other reactions – both overt and covert.

Lesson: The brain is extremely good at filling in the gaps, i.e. making assumptions.

People do not collaborate well in the midst of all of that. Their unmet individual needs and their lifelong habits keep them from trusting and sharing with others. Innovation is not happening because people are afraid of being criticised or having their new ideas ridiculed. Those fears further shut down creativity and the ability to be innovative. Results suffer.

The problems are complex. Although the source of it all is becoming much clearer, unfortunately, the solutions most organisations turn to only attempt to solve the symptoms and never get near the root of the problems.

Leadership – In-House, Together

One of the common methods of attempting to solve some of those problems in organisations is to send leaders on a leadership development programme and expect them to come back and fix the problems in their teams and departments.

Imagine you have a colleague named Bob. He's a relatively new department head, and the groups in his department often miss target dates and produce work full of mistakes. Other department heads on the management team blame Bob and his lack of leadership skills. Bob has never had any formal managerial or leadership training, so the company sends him on a leadership course.

Bob has a fantastic time. He realises how much he didn't know, and he learns a number of tools. He feels inspired, empowered and excited to implement those great new tools as soon as he gets back to the office. Over the weekend, he creates a great plan for his department, and on Monday morning, he informs the group leaders what the changes are going to be.

But it backfires! The team leaders nod, pay lip service, and as soon as Bob has left the meeting room, they tell each other, "There you go, I told you so; he's been on a course and wants to change everything. Let's just agree, keep a low profile, and he'll be back to normal in couple of weeks."

And so it goes, two weeks later, everything is back to normal – course forgotten.

It's painful to hear the stories from some of the leaders we've trained. They return to their workplace inspired and full of enthusiasm, and then they fail spectacularly at implementing the new tools we taught them. Even though they believe in the new approaches and can see how useful they are, the leaders cannot find a way to use them consistently in their work. It's as if an invisible force keeps them from succeeding.

That invisible force is real. It's called culture – the company culture – and it's a powerful force that, more often than not, will resist an individual's attempts to change and will try, instead, to keep the status quo intact.

Culture is powerful. It not only eats strategy for breakfast (as the well-known quote tells us), it also determines which changes will stick and which ones won't.

Culture is created by groups of people – a collection of human brains. Again, understanding the brain helps us understand the basis of human interaction. Combined with the study of systems thinking, we can learn a lot about culture, how it impacts each person in it and how we can all impact and shift the culture itself.

We know that for change to take place, there needs to be involvement and engagement from everyone involved in the change. If a leader is going to change his or her approach to leading the team, the team members need to understand and buy into it because, as the people being led, they have a part to play. Leadership happens in relationship, not in isolation. Team members need to align with the change and then work together on shaping and implementing it. They need to understand and help to design the why, the what, and the how of it. It is not just leader development; it is both leader development and culture change, together.

Why This Book

The aim of this book is not to provide a simplistic solution to your complex problems. We aim to provide some more understanding of what is really going on in an organisation of people. Secondly, we want to share with you the possibilities of addressing widespread problems with widespread solutions that address the core of what is really going on. We propose an integrated approach based on neuroscience and systems thinking that allows time for real change to happen.

In short form our proposed approach is this:

- **Start with training.** Train the leaders at the top, together. Use training techniques optimised for engagement and learning. Help them understand the social brain – what is going on individually with people and what happens when people are working together – so they can better manage and lead their people. Give them some tools to use and behaviours to practise that leverage the knowledge about brains and systems. Training leaders together creates a common language, leverages the systemic nature of people and gives the message to the rest of the organisation that "We are in this together." Leadership is not an individualistic event.

- **Support the changes.** Individual coaching, used in the context of the programme, will support individual learning and behaviour change. Even more important is support provided by systemic team coaching, which helps the collective embed new behaviours; this is where we see changes making a real difference.

- **Roll-out**. As the leaders start to learn and shift their behaviours, roll out a similar training throughout the organisation. Create common understanding throughout about the peculiarities and magnificence of the human brain. Support that learning with coaching and team coaching. Create a culture where the brain matters, where caring for the system – the whole – matters.

- **Create safety.** We need the safety of being able to fail so we can actually try something new. As leaders try the new behaviours first, they will create safety for others to do the same. Leaders and managers throughout the organisation can help create a safe environment so that people can do things differently.

- **Allow time.** Humans take time to change; we need repetitive practice and time to re-train the brain in new behaviours.

We have seen that as team members keep the brain's tendencies in mind, they can truly learn to trust each other and to collaborate effectively. Add some understanding about how creativity works and innovation will follow. We know that more collaboration and innovation lead to better results.

The Sekhmed Team

To bring our neuroscience and systems thinking lessons to life, we have created a company, Sekhmed, its management team, and an IT product named Sekhmed Software. The Sekhmed Division is mostly self-contained but is owned by a large organisation we refer to as The Corporation. It is fictitious but is based on reality. We think you will recognise many of the characters in the team, and you will probably recognise many of the problems they face. We will use the Sekhmed team throughout the book to help demonstrate our proposed approach to change.

Notes from the Introduction

- The brain creates habits. We rely on habits in order to function every day.

- The brain is not hardwired. We can learn to do things differently.

- The brain focuses on survival. This drives us to be protective of our needs and fearful of perceived threats.

- The brain is a social brain. We are designed to be in relationship with others.

- The brain is extremely good at filling in the gaps. We constantly make assumptions.

- In the Western world, we are trained to be individualistic and we create habits based on that worldview. We can become more team focused, but it will require us to change our thinking and habits.

- Leadership development, personal development and culture change must happen in parallel and inside the organisation.

- Learning takes time.

PART 1
The Sekhmed Story

1. Crisis Time at Sekhmed Medical Software

George walked down the corridor to his boss's office. He'd been feeling uneasy about things recently and wondered if he was in trouble. Was Kate going to fire him? But surely that was impossible. He'd started Sekhmed Medical Software himself, and he was still a much-needed and integral part of this company. Just because he sold Sekhmed to The Corporation and was now just an employee in a management position shouldn't matter. Should it?

Kate Alderton sat at her desk, waiting for George to arrive. She was completely stressed out and feeling unusually frazzled. After proving her worth as a young leader in the manufacturing division of The Corporation, she'd been chosen to head up their Sekhmed division and turn things around. But a year later, despite the changes she'd already made, things were no better.

Kate knew things needed to change drastically now, and she had just been told by Head Office that she had one more year to make it happen. For the first time in her career, she felt lost. She had asked George to come to see her, hoping that as the founder of Sekhmed, he'd know something that might help her.

Clamping down on his feeling of dread, George entered Kate's office with his habitual, amicable smile. He was surprised to find that his normally cool-under-pressure boss seemed ready to break down. George, who was usually a bit wary of Kate, actually felt sorry for her when he saw her in such an emotional state.

Kate took a deep breath and composed herself. "I've just been chewed out by head office because the Sekhmed customer satisfaction survey was worse than last year. That makes it a four-year downward trend. And profits were also down. Head Office was certain there was a connection."

Her voice was strained. "George, I know we don't always see eye-to-eye, but I really need your help. Can you talk me through what's going on here?"

So he wasn't about to be fired! More than a little taken aback by seeing his dynamic boss in such a fragile state, George decided to focus completely on Kate and on what she was saying – for the sake of the whole business. Clearly she needed his help. The fact that she had called on him gave him a boost and completely wiped out his own personal worries.

"Sure. What do you need to know?"

Kate let her thoughts spill out with all their frustration. "There are so many things to tackle. The management team seems to be falling apart and blaming each other for the problems, and I cannot get to the core of what's really wrong. Is it personal vendettas in the management team spiralling out of control and ultimately affecting customers? Is it really poor customer service? Is it poor software?

"I know that the last systems software release didn't go well. Despite all the in-house testing by the developers and the Maintenance group, customers have been reporting so many bugs in the updated software – problems in areas that have long been stable. That's really disturbing."

Kate had spent the last year trying to assess the problems that had shown up in previous customer service reports and had made a few changes. She had moved the Customer Service department out of Maintenance and into the Sales Department because Iris, as Head of Sales, was so great with people. Iris really knew the ins and outs of pleasing customers and was good at training others in it too.

"This year's report shows that while customers reported feeling that they were better cared for by the Customer Service people, they didn't think they were getting their problems solved in anything like a timely manner. So it seems that moving Customer Service into Sales was a waste of effort. What's the good of having nicer Customer Service people if it doesn't end up making a difference?"

George could have told her why, but he decided to hear Kate out.

Kate ran a hand through her hair. "There's a strange dynamic between the Sales team and the rest of the division." Sales were a tight-knit group and relatively happy. They were clearly proud of their numbers, and Iris was fiercely protective of her team; she wouldn't let anyone speak badly about them.

Kate didn't know much about Iris Thistle because she usually got a bit of a cold shoulder from her. She avoided Iris and digging into that situation, but she realised she was going to have to face what was happening in Sales.

"Sales figures are high," Kate continued. "I know the sales people have great relationships with hospitals and medical labs where our software is used. But so many of those sales are dependent on specialty options asked for by the customers. There don't seem to be any straightforward contracts where customers buy a standard package. There are always special options requiring extra development work."

"I'm not sure if problems are being driven by Sales agreeing to any options the customers want, if the Applications group isn't able to come through on those special requests, if the variants are destabilizing the software platform or if there are so many problems that Maintenance can't catch them all ... Was that the way it always was – so many options made available to customers?"

"In our startup days, it was all about that," George told her with pride. "We built our reputation on how we could customise, optimise and deliver in a short time. It was so much easier then. And we still like working that way. But all the QA procedures and standards and processes slow us down so much."

George remembered how much simpler things were in those first few years. Maybe they should have stayed a small company. But then he wouldn't have been able to sell Sekhmed and create that nest egg of his, most of which was currently invested in yet another startup. When the new company was sold, he would be home free, fully retired and living well. But for now, his money was invested and he still needed to work. And he cared about Sekhmed; it was still his baby to some extent. He needed to help here. He couldn't just bide his time. He looked at Kate with more attention and a resolve to be more helpful.

Kate thought again about the customer service issues: too many software bugs, lower profits... Then she shifted the focus of the conversation to Maintenance. Was it really them who missed all those bugs? She could not imagine that ex-military run-a-tight-ship Frank Peters would sign off on software that was so unstable. "Tell me about Frank and Maintenance. Frank is so attentive to detail. How could they have signed off on software that had all those bugs in it?"

"Well ... ," George started cautiously. "I think they didn't expect to have to test all the platform routines again. Mostly they focus on the newer applications. And I know that Frank is always upset that there are so many new little applications here and there. He thinks Iris kowtows to customers way too much. And something has happened in Maintenance. I think they have lost some team spirit or something. They did not like it that their friends from Customer Service were moved. They seemed to lose touch with customers. I guess they could be angry and taking it out on the whole company."

"So you're saying that my moving the Customer Service team to work under Iris has caused problems with the guys in Maintenance?"

"Well," George reasoned, "they had a pretty tight relationship, and they could discuss issues over coffee." He gave a little laugh. "I used to go to their offices, and I couldn't believe the technical conversations they were enjoying over coffee! I do not think that happens any more. They lost their enthusiasm. Those coffee conversations are much less spirited these days. In fact, that whole department seems a bit depressed. I also think they're resentful that there's a QA person who's not part of their department. They think their jobs might be threatened."

Kate raised her eyebrows in surprise. "OK. We can move them back if that is what they need. Let's come back to that. You mentioned QA. Let us focus on that. I made the decision to bring a QA person in because it seemed to me that this company was at a stage where that was needed.

"Sekhmed is no longer a startup. People seem to not recognise that. This company is big enough that there needs to be clearer QA processes and more documented communication between Development, Maintenance and Customer Service. Cedric Smith is a hotshot in QA; he's got a black belt in Six Sigma, he's bright and he knows the ropes. The Corporation is paying for him – what a deal for us! Are you saying that wasn't a good idea? I thought people liked Cedric; he's such a likeable guy!"

Kate felt even more bewildered. How could all her good intentions and changes over the past year have been so off-mark?

George gave a half-smile. "Well, we do like to think of ourselves as quick and nimble like a startup. I'll give you that. And you're probably right, we might need a little more QA help. But I think maybe Cedric isn't the right guy."

"How do you mean?"

George shrugged. "Cedric is friendly, but he's a bit young and he backs down so quickly. He doesn't have the assertiveness needed for someone in that role to get these more seasoned professionals to listen to him. It's pretty clear that Frank doesn't pay any attention to him." He didn't want to tell Kate that Frank called Cedric a weakling and worse behind closed doors. "I think Cedric doesn't measure up to Frank's idea of a "leader."" You know Frank's military style. It doesn't leave much room for softer-spoken guys like Cedric. So he thinks Cedric has nothing to offer, despite all his credentials."

Kate nodded her agreement. She could help Cedric with his assertiveness problem. Assertiveness training was easy to find. "But I really don't think everything will be fixed just by helping Cedric to be more assertive. There's a lot more to it than just QA. QA shouldn't have to fix deeper problems."

She turned her attention to the core of the software. "Tell me about Paul Danwood and the Platform Department. That was one place I thought was stable and completely reliable. But these reports show that there are all kinds of bugs that are coming from the platform itself! I don't get it. I know I'm not the world's expert on IT, but I know the difference between the platform software and applications. Why are there now bugs in the platform that weren't there before?"

George frowned. "I don't understand what has happened with Paul. I had groomed him to lead the Software Platform Department. He got that job when I took the lead role in the Applications Department. I thought it would all work out really well. We have a great working relationship. I was sure he was going to do a great job. But now he seems lost."

Kate looked thoughtful. "What does that have to do with new bugs being created over there?"

George shrugged a little defensively. "We have all these different requests coming in from Iris's Sales team, and the Applications team love them. Occasionally, we notice that if there were a few shifts in the platform, our applications would be easier and quicker to create. So ... sometimes ... I have asked Paul or his people to make those changes."

Kate was beside herself. "Are you telling me that you've asked for special changes in the platform that weren't strictly necessary? Changes that might have destabilised the system?" She brought herself back under control. "And did I hear that you might have also gone around Paul to ask his team members directly?"

George looked sheepish. "Yes, I have asked for various things from Paul and his team. And yes, they might have had an impact on the platform performance. But that's not my fault. It's Paul's job to make sure it works or to tell me that it can't. That should be his number one priority – to keep up to date on what everyone is doing and make sure it can all work together."

Kate let out a long breath. "OK. I get the picture." Everybody knew that Paul and his team members would never say "No" to George. He was like a father figure to Paul. There was a lot here that George wasn't taking responsibility for, and it was clear he liked to blame others. But she chose not to call him on it – yet.

"Tell me about the relationship between all these sales and special applications being ordered by customers, and you guys over there in Applications. It seems to me that despite Iris creating lots of sales, some of those things she agrees to don't create profit. It seems to take a lot of time to create these special favours for special customers. I don't get it."

George didn't try to hide his sarcasm. "Well, it would help if Iris was better at knowing what was profitable and what wasn't."

Kate felt her frustration mounting, but she managed to check it. Earlier, she'd been feeling devastated and pretty emotional. But talking with George had helped her to let off steam, and she was starting to feel more in control of herself. A good thing too: she needed every bit of that control right now, so she wouldn't blow up at George for the way he was being so irresponsible.

She decided to ignore George's tone. "We've sent some of your guys on sales calls with Iris's sales people specifically to help straighten that out. But it seems they've just encouraged more sales and new functionality. We were trying to create some alliances between Sales and Applications so as to eliminate some of the extreme specialisations, but that's obviously backfired."

"Yeah, well ...," George shrugged off any responsibility. "The guys like that fancy stuff. They love the challenges. It's hard for them to see what's profitable or not. I think Iris should know more."

George was blaming others again. Kate decided it was time to challenge him. "It seems like some of this should be your job, George, to know what's profitable, don't you think?"

"Well, that's what I've tried to say at several of our recent Executive Management Team meetings." It was George's turn to explode. "But Iris shoots me down and she's better at arguing. She says she's better at dealing with customers. She brings in the bacon and that seems to trump everything! She plays the revenue card and threatens that we'll lose all our customers to those new companies who are cheaper and more competitive, like we used to be. And everyone always agrees with her and no one listens to me."

Kate recognised the truth in what he said. She and the team seemed to bend pretty far when it came to letting Iris have her way. How was she going to be able to manage Iris?

"Besides," George added, a little less forcefully now. "Maybe the real problem isn't that she's selling those special apps. It might be more about the timeline. Iris needs to realise that it takes time to code, test, re-test and document new software – and do the QA work."

Kate couldn't disagree with him, but she was coming to the end of her tether. "What do you recommend, George? We've got a lot of entangled problems here."

He'd been unfair to blame Kate for being an incompetent leader. The problems were far more complicated than he'd realised. "I'm sorry, Kate. I really don't know what to do. I think this is why I'm no longer running the company. I'm more of a software developer than a corporate leader. You're well trained. I'm sure you'll think of something. And I want you to know that you've got my support, seriously."

They looked at each other in silence for several seconds. Then Kate nodded slowly, acknowledging his words. Well, at least it now felt like George was on her side, which was comforting. "Thanks, George, it's good to know you're an ally."

Kate closed her door behind George and sat down to think. The meeting with him had been really valuable. For one thing, it had helped her to get all the problems out of her head. She'd also got some input from George. But most importantly, she'd discovered that George might unintentionally be undermining progress at Sekhmed.

Notes from Chapter 1

- Sekhmed software is a division of a larger organisation called The Corporation. Kate is the head of the division, and George is the original creator of the software and company that launched it. Those two plus four others comprise the management team.

- The Sekhmed division is experiencing a four year downtrend in customer satisfaction, and profits are dropping as well.

- They have problems that are typical of a small but growing organisation: attempts at developing processes and varying levels of commitment – even some actions that might seem like undermining others' efforts.

- They have problems typical of any organisation: personal conflicts; different objectives; teams fighting each other creating silos; some individuals who are too aggressive, others who are not assertive enough.

2. Trying to Fix the Problems

When Kate finally stretched her arms and let out a long sigh, she realised it was almost dark outside. She'd been staring out of her office window, deep in thought, since George had left her office. But at least she now had a better idea of what might be going on in her executive team and had come up with some possible fixes to the problems.

George, as the founder of the company, felt entitled to do whatever he wanted, but he wasn't taking any responsibility for his actions; he dumped it on everyone else. It was clear that he still cared about Sekhmed, though, and somehow, she would have to get him to see his impact and take more responsibility.

Iris, the dynamic head of Sales, had taken on the role of protector of her department. She believed her team was superior to all the others because they kept the money flowing in. Maybe they did, but in fact, many of the sales they made actually created much more detailed work that was leading to instability in the platform and reducing profits overall. They wouldn't say "No" to any customers. Kate noticed her own fear of the woman and her team. Some kind of confrontation would have to take place over there, and she would definitely need help with that.

Paul, the head of Platform, still idolised his mentor, George. He would do anything to stay on George's good side, and he wasn't managing his people well. Did he have what it takes to be a great leader? He wasn't exactly demonstrating good leadership, and he clearly had trouble setting boundaries and saying "No" when he needed to.

Cedric might be a star in the field of quality assurance and generally liked by people, but that didn't mean he knew how to get people to implement his quality policies and procedures. She had thought he was going to be the saviour of the quality issues. That failure was so disappointing and she knew it wasn't exactly Cedric's fault.

Then there was military man Frank and his Maintenance department. She still wasn't sure what was going on over there, but she did get the sense that two of her attempts at making things better, moving Customer Service to Sales and bringing in a QA guy from The Corporation, may have angered that whole department.

Kate thought through her plan again. She'd start by connecting with Frank and figure out if moving Customer Services back to his department would help. And then she would organise some leadership training for the department heads.

***

Now what, Kate thought in despair six months later, cradling her head in her hands. She'd been so pleased with the leadership programme she'd attended and had returned buoyed up with plans and ideas of how she'd handle things.

But having given her plan her best shot and seen that fall apart, she was at a loss to know where to go next. The dream she'd secretly been nurturing, of joyfully sending off her next report to Head Office showing an improvement in the last quarter's figures and knowing that her team was now working well together, had been stillborn. She felt a real sense of loss for the success that would clearly not be hers.

Frank and George had declined the offer of any kind of training programme. They both felt they were old enough and wise enough not to need any soft skills training.

Paul had attended a management course and he, too, had come back full of enthusiasm about his experience. Armed with his new skills, he'd tried to create clearer roles and responsibilities in the Platform department. He'd been really optimistic too, and she'd had real hopes that he'd be able to turn around the relationships and his department. She'd seen his plans and had been impressed by the matrix of roles and responsibilities he'd drawn up.

But three weeks after the course, nothing much had changed. "It's all fallen flat," he'd later told her, frustrated and confused. "The team members complain that I'm micromanaging them, and I can see they're just paying lip service to the new structures." When she'd overheard Paul telling George that he'd stopped trying to use his new tools and heard them agreeing that these new tools didn't work in a place like Sekhmed, her heart had sunk.

At least things were going well for Cedric. He had received some personal development coaching to work on his assertiveness and had learned that if he was going to be successful at implementing his strategies, he was going to have to be willing to be seen as something other than "the nice guy." It was tough, but his coach was challenging and supportive.

Cedric had started demonstrating more and more strength of character each week. "I know I've gained some allies in the various programming groups, especially in the Applications department," he told Kate with a touch of pride. "One of the three groups has become a big fan of QA."

But Kate could see that the other two groups were against it, which was creating a rift in the Applications department. And she realised now that when she and George had publically praised the pro-QA group for taking on the new QA procedures, they had unwittingly deepened the rift. It seemed they were going two steps forward, one step back, she thought in despair.

Kate had been observing her management team discretely – more of a tuning in than a spying on. She had noticed how Frank rolled his eyes at Cedric's attempt at stepping into leadership and how he supported his own team members in mocking Cedric. She had seen that the few people in the Maintenance team who really saw the benefit of Cedric's QA work were afraid to support it because of Frank's dislike for the guy, and that this had caused some strain throughout the Maintenance group.

Because Kate had learned about the importance of relationship in her leadership programme, she tried to implement her new relationship building skills with Iris, but to little effect, because Iris was suspicious.

Kate started being more curious and tried asking more questions. That backfired, particularly with lead-like-a-military-officer Frank. But she was successful in listening to him about the Customer Service team and decided to move them back to the Maintenance department. That, at least, seemed to raise spirits a bit in Maintenance, but it also created more problems with Iris, who felt it was an insult to take them away from her department – she had been doing a really good job leading them.

Kate felt like she just couldn't win!

These are typical problems in a company. Not just in IT but in many companies. And the typical approach is for the leader to try to fix them.

Kate is trying to solve all of the problems herself. She thinks that's what she was hired for – and it was. But she has a resource available to her that she's not using, and that's the Executive Management Team as a whole.

In Part 2, we will look at this team in a little more detail, using what we have learned from neuroscience and systems thinking to understand what's going on with the team.

Neuroscience will help us more with the individuals and why they behave the way they do. Their behaviour might be frustrating, but it is fairly predictable and not at all surprising, given what we now know about human brains and how we react to one another.

Then we look at systems theory and apply that to the Sekhmed team to get some more insights on the team and its collective behaviours.

In Part 3, we will discuss a completely different approach to this set of problems, which takes into account the social brain.

But for now, let's look at what's going on in the Sekhmed team from a slightly more informed standpoint by using neuroscience and a systems approach.

Notes from Chapter 2

- The boss tries to fix everything herself (like a super-hero), but it doesn't work.

- Sending leaders away to training programmes inspires the individual but doesn't ensure they can implement what they learned.

- People decide that "those tools don't work here" and give up.

- Fixing people or problems doesn't change a culture

- Coaching is helpful to some extent, but changes in one person can create reactions in others, which may worsen the original problem.

PART 2
Neuroscience

3. Introduction to Neuroscience

In order to understand what's going on in the Sekhmed team, or any team or organisation these days, we need to incorporate what neuroscience tells us about the human brain and how we operate. We will show you what's happening with the various Sekhmed members, and why things seem to be getting worse, even after some great training for a few of the executives. Then we'll add in some systemic thinking and put together a new approach for addressing Sekhmed's issues.

Recent neuroscience research provides a wealth of information about how our brains work. Most notable, in our opinion, is the discovery that the brain is a social brain more than it is a computing machine. So much of our brain's real estate is dedicated to being in relationship and to responding to stimuli from other people in our environment.

Many of the functions in the brain evolved thousands of years ago to keep people safe and thriving. As our world changed, we naturally adapted those brain functions to our current social environments and our interactions with each other, many of which take place at work.

The brain is extremely complicated and complex. Here we present just a few functions of the brain that we think are critical to understanding what happens to us when we interact with others in our everyday lives. This is not a neuroscience textbook, so we are taking a fairly light approach and certainly not trying to give the full picture of the brain.

The Drive for Survival

It's essential to know something about the brain's focus on survival. There are a number of structures in the inner part of the brain that are collectively called the Limbic System. All animals, even the tiniest worms, have a limbic system. Its function is survival: to help us acquire sustenance and make sure we stay safe from predators; i.e. to eat and reproduce, but not get eaten or injured. It gets a little more complicated for mammals, as survival must include the care of others in the tribe because the tribe is also essential for survival. Most mammals, and humans in particular, cannot survive very well on their own. Children need to be nurtured until they are at an age where they can take care of themselves. It's much more efficient to hunt together, and there's safety in numbers. So belonging – and some other social factors – is also an essential element of our survival.

Imagine our ancestors living on the savannahs in Africa. They were hunter-gatherers, living in small family groups, clans and tribes. Their world was physically more challenging than ours, and there were actual, physical threats all around, such as large predators, poisonous bugs and berries, hostile neighbours and so on.

The limbic system scans the environment and is alert to various threats and also possibilities of sustenance. If there is something of note, the limbic system makes sure we notice. If there's a threat, neurotransmitters and hormones are released in our system to make our nervous system kick in; adrenaline gives us energy to flee or fight – two standard fear responses – while other chemicals shut down other functions like digestion. Our heart rate increases, our eyesight gets sharper and we have more energy – all so that we can respond quickly. These reactions are extremely fast and they are NOT conscious. It is not something you need to analyse, think about or discuss. Your body just reacts.

Imagine one of our ancestors walking in the bush, hearing the grass rustle. She instantly feels threatened, and adrenaline gives her the urgent message to run away or to climb a tree, because it MIGHT be danger. If it was a sabre-tooth tiger, she has just ensured that her genes will survive another day. If it was just the wind in the grass ... well, she still gets to live another day! Better to look a little foolish than be dead. Her limbic system worked well. The next day, she goes to collect berries in the woods. For this action, the limbic system rewards her with dopamine, a feel-good chemical that is released when she does something that ensures survival. It turns out that running from the rustle of the grass is more important than gathering food. There is five times more circuitry dedicated to the fear of threats than there is for the desire for sustenance. As humans, we run from threats and walk towards rewards.

Now, fast-forward several millennia. Here we are in a super-complex environment where physical threats are fewer and further between, but our world is full of different worries: social and emotional threats relating to our status and what other people think of us. However, our limbic system hasn't developed much. It cannot distinguish between physical threats and social threats. And there are social threats everywhere. Whenever you receive a stimulus (see, hear or smell something) the probability is still five times higher that you will react as if this is a threat! Your amygdala triggers the release of adrenaline into your body, your heart rate increases, your mouth gets dry, and the desire to fight, flee, freeze or appease causes you to react before you even know it.

When you see someone yawning during your presentation (especially if it's your boss), you are more likely to interpret that as a threat to you than just think that your colleague needs to get more rest.

The limbic system is ever vigilant – on the lookout for threats to our survival and always ready to give us the signal "spring into action" if it seems necessary. And, on a smaller scale, it's always looking for opportunities to enhance our survival and get a dopamine reward. The limbic system is fast, always on, and ready to react far quicker than the speed of thought.

It is specifically monitoring for threats and the possibility of rewards in these limbic triggers (and possibly others that neuroscientists haven't yet clarified):

- **Belonging:** To be cast out of the tribe is to die. We need to belong to a tribe and make sure that we do not risk losing that connection. Humans cannot survive long on their own. Children must be cared for for many years.

- **Status:** Once in a tribe, it's important to be relevant in that tribe. Even though we belong to a tribe, we still have a drive to be "better than" within the tribe. Our tribe also needs to be better than our rival tribes to ensure our survival.

- **Fairness:** We have a strong need for fairness. The brain's reaction to unfairness is visceral; we feel it deeply. The reaction is quite similar to disgust. We will monitor for fairness pertaining to ourselves but also for fairness to others.

- **Certainty:** We need to know what is happening and why. We will survive more easily if we know what to expect from our environment, if we know where sustenance will come from and when and where threats might arise. This drives us to control our environment and creates great discomfort in dealing with the unknown.

- **Autonomy:** We have a need to be able to choose for ourselves what we want and what we do. If others try to control us, we react and push back.

The limbic system causes us to react with fear any time any of these areas is threatened. If we are insulted, demoted, fired, or come in second, that can create a status threat. Managers trying to control their direct reports will create limbic threat reactions. Any change initiative will create uncertainty and perceived threats.

Just think about spectators at a sports event to envision some of these reactions on full display. People easily form tribes by stating their allegiance to a particular team. It's very easy to see the sense of tribe play out: *we are a tribe, and the others are the enemies.* We are happy, thanks to doses of dopamine entering our system, when "we" win, and especially when "we" are on top. We have to be treated fairly; just watch what happens to a crowd when a referee makes an unfair call, and see how people react. The need for fairness is very strong.

It might be helpful to know that these limbic factors can balance one another. If we experience status threats, the limbic system will try to remedy this and restore balance by creating rewards elsewhere, perhaps by creating some belonging. Being losers – of low status – together is better than being a loser alone.

It's also important to know that reactions beget more reactions. Imagine the following situation:

Alex, preoccupied with his own problems, passes Jane without saying "Good morning." Jane immediately thinks Alex is angry with her. Her reaction is to make an angry remark – a fight response – which, to Alex, comes out of nowhere. He is bewildered but ignores the comment because his limbic system generates a freeze reaction.

This can escalate out of control as limbic reactions keep reacting to limbic reactions. Often, reactions will take the form of revenge: plotting a punishment of sorts.

But let's not paint the limbic system as all evil or bad. It does provide us with a great service even in this day and age.

Imagine being half awake one morning. Your alarm goes off, but you don't have to get up quite yet. You hit the snooze button, and you're enjoying those last few minutes of dozy sleep. Then suddenly you realise it's today that you have to take an early flight to that all-important meeting! Boom. Your system is instantly flooded with adrenalin, you fly out of bed, call the taxi, zip through your bathroom routine, get dressed in world-record speed, and you are out of the door faster than ever before. Thanks to the limbic system, you've been able to tap into warp speed, and you make it to your flight, even if it does take you twenty minutes of the taxi ride to calm down and flush all the chemicals out of your system. We can be thankful for this amazing part of our brain that really does save the day from time to time.

Mirror Neurons and Empathy

It's important to understand a little about mirror neurons. These are specialised neurons in the brain that remove distinctions between oneself and others. When we see something happening to someone else, we can react as if the event happened to us. So we can get a limbic reaction, say a fairness reaction, if we see someone else being treated unfairly. This is why films, plays and television can pull our emotions around so much. We have the gift of being moved by others' plights and successes. Similarly, if a colleague is mistreated by our boss, we could react just as much as, or perhaps more than, that colleague.

Error Detection (Part of the Limbic System)

The limbic system is always looking for an "error" in the environment, a situation where something different from the expected happens. This difference could be as big as an explosion outside the office, or as small as someone not saying his usual "Hello" when passing us in the hallway. "What's wrong with him?," we react, as the brain jumps to conclusions and creates a new assumption in the absence of information.

Conclusions and assumptions are a necessary part of adapting, and the brain is good at it. Depending on our view of the world, the conclusions or assumptions might be "positive" or they might be "negative." Remember that we have five times more circuitry to assume something is a threat than to look for a reward, so it's much more likely we'll interpret the worst. But wrong assumptions still give us certainty, and being certain and wrong is better than dealing with the unknown.

We actually do have a lot of control over our interpretations – that part can be conscious. We can re-train the limbic system to react or to not react, and we can build habits about how we react to certain stimuli. This is one of the ways we can help ourselves from being too reactive and interpreting everything as a threat to our existence (you might know some people like that …).

Let us look at how that works.

The Human Benefit – the Prefrontal Cortex

Fortunately, we humans have a special asset, another structure in our brains that helps us to manage these animal survival reactions. It's called the prefrontal cortex, or PFC, and it sits at the front of the brain above the eyes. Among the PFC's multitude of human functions is the ability to manage the limbic system and even to retrain it.

Imagine standing in front of a large group of people for the very first time. The limbic system is most likely to see the audience as a threat, and it will tell us to run off the stage or force us to freeze. But if we stand on a stage a number of times, we will learn that people in the audience are not going to attack us, in fact, they

49

might even be friendly. Those experiences re-train the limbic system through repetition. The PFC can also re-train the limbic system by changing our attitude or opinion. So Alex didn't say, "Hello" this morning; my limbic system is telling me to go and pick a fight with him, but my PFC can remind me that he's going through a difficult time right now, and his lack of a hello has nothing to do with me. We can re-train our limbic systems to find the best in people, to think of the positive, to assume good intent. It can uncover the unconscious conclusions and assumptions that the limbic system helped us make, and it can change them.

The PFC can help us see the difference between what we've made up (Alex is mad at me) and what is real (Alex is having a difficult time).

Consciously Focused Attention

The PFC has many functions:

- Managing limbic reactions so we stay calm instead of reacting

- Staying focused and pointing our attention. This is an essential part of being human. We can choose to ignore the rustling in the leaves and instead focus on the task at hand

- Keeping us disciplined to keep going when the going gets tough

- Keeping us focused on goals and tuning out things that compete for our attention

- Deciding whether to focus our attention on tasks or on the people around us who are looking to us for connection

- Helping us delay gratification

- Problem solving

- Logic

- Goal setting and planning

50

- Self-awareness and self-reflection

The ability to point our own attention is quite remarkable. We can choose our focus. Most often, we don't do it consciously; instead we often let our environment or our limbic system pull our attention this way and that.

We will develop habits of where we put our attention by what we focus on daily, what we like or don't like, what we want or don't want, possibilities or problems. The PFC can help us do this consciously. Without that conscious focus, the limbic system will force our attention to what we should be afraid of.

The Limited PFC

One of the biggest problems we have as humans is that our amazing PFC is slow, weak and lazy. The PFC is much slower than the limbic system, and it tires more easily. From the brain's perspective, the most efficient way to operate is to react quickly, often from fear for the sake of self-preservation, and use what's already stored as a habit. Then the PFC doesn't have to engage at all. Our brain doesn't like to make decisions if it doesn't have to.

However, if we want to be more conscious and intentional in our actions, we need to pay attention, engage the PFC, and consciously focus attention. But that takes a little more effort until it, too, is a habit. The PFC is like a muscle that needs to be exercised and strengthened, and we generally don't work it; there isn't much that teaches us how to exercise our PFCs.

The PFC can only handle one thing at a time. We cannot multitask. If the PFC is busy managing emotions – maybe stopping us from yelling at someone in a meeting – we won't have a lot of energy and space left for problem solving or forward planning.

If we're focused on a task, and we're then surprised with a threat from the environment, it's most likely that the limbic response to a threat will take over because the PFC was too busy focusing to manage that reaction.

Imagine yourself working really hard to not react to the person across the table who makes you very angry. Your PFC will be engaged in calming yourself, and its capacity to do other things will be diminished. You will have a harder time focusing in the meeting.

If we're distracted by disturbances at home, we'll have less ability to focus at work. If we're at the end of the quarter, and we've got to land a few more sales, our focus will probably be on sales, and we might miss the entries in the calendar that say it's our child's birthday, or forget to eat, which further diminishes the PFC operating capacity.

To keep our PFC in good working order, we need good sleep and good nutrition. If we're undernourished or sleep deprived, we will be less able to focus on work and less able to control our reactive nature when something shows up that the limbic system interprets as a threat. What's more, every time the limbic system reacts to a threat, our body produces cortisol, which is toxic to the body. We were meant to experience stress, adrenaline and cortisol in small doses. Frequent occurrences of cortisol actually diminish our memory and the capacity of the PFC.

We can also strengthen the PFC by practices including mindfulness, a form of meditation. A lot of research is showing that we can grow our PFC and therefore the capacity of all of our PFC functions if we spend some time in mindfulness training. Mindfulness is a practice of non-judgemental awareness. It trains the brain to notice what's going on without reacting, and it's one way to overcome habits we've developed of allowing our limbic system to take over and react with fear.

Choosing to Focus on People

A recent study (Reference: Sukhvinder Obhi) shows that when humans experience a sense of power, their mirror neurons shut off. Mirror neurons help us to relate to others and to have empathy. The study shows that when people get a promotion, for example, they have less concern for their previous colleagues. Indeed, it is a fairly well-known complaint amongst professionals that when a colleague is promoted, he or she seems to change and become arrogant or distant. The study tells us that we can still have empathy along with feelings of power, but we need to train ourselves to pay attention to others and our impact on them. The PFC needs to engage and consciously choose to focus on relationships.

Similarly, another area where leaders need to pay attention is the pull between task and relationship. The brain is not naturally capable of focussing on both at the same time.

Multitasking is a myth; we never multitask, we can only switch focus. That could happen more quickly for some people than others and might look like multitasking.

We need to train ourselves to switch focus between these two essential parts of leadership. If we get task focused, we will start treating other people like objects that can be moved around and manipulated. It's well proven that this doesn't work well; it creates morale issues. If we stop paying attention to what they need, it almost guarantees that they will respond with limbic reactions. Very few people would want to work for a boss or with colleagues who are hundred percent task focused. On the other hand, if we are only focused on relationship, we might not get any tasks accomplished. We need to use our PFC to focus our attention on both task and relationship. Leaders, in particular, need both.

Efficiency and the Habit-Making Machine

Because the PFC is not very strong, the brain will turn something into a habit or pattern as quickly as possible. We won't need to spend all of our PFC energy focusing on how to do something if we already know how to do it. However, it often doesn't take much to create a habit out of a series of actions, and this can get us into trouble, for example, if we unconsciously assume that something will repeatedly be the same after we've only seen it happen once.

Habits are created by the brain getting the data out of the limited PFC and pushing it into the habit storage area, called the Basal Ganglia (that's plural). The Basal Ganglia store memories about how to ride a horse or a bicycle, so we can do it again years later without having to re-learn. We might need to polish our muscle control, but the basic functions are still there. The Basal Ganglia also help us remember how to eat breakfast, brush our teeth, get dressed and drive a car, as well as how we get to work, etc. If we had to think about each of those things consciously, we would be exhausted before we even got to work. So the Basal Ganglia save us a lot of energy. It's an efficient system and it works well. The Basal Ganglia try to detect patterns as soon as possible and then the brain relies on those patterns. It's the way habits are created and also a way that assumptions are established.

Example: Imagine the first day in your new job. You observe one of your new colleagues come out of the boss's office, upset. You then see another person come out of the office and he also is visibly upset. Your brain has already noticed the relationship, and is on its way to establishing a pattern and assumption: this boss upsets people. Without thinking, that becomes a "truth" in your mind.

Habits, by the very nature of how they are stored in the Basal Ganglia and not the PFC, are unconscious by definition. And this gets us in trouble. We have all kinds of habits: some might be physical, like how we choose to drive to work. We also have emotional habits, such as how we react to certain situations. And we have social habits like saying, "Good morning" and "How are you?" Often, we say, "Hello, how are you?" and "I'm fine," without thinking. They are habits that we barely notice any more unless they go missing, as with the earlier example when Jane passed Alex and he didn't say "Good morning." Jane's error detectors fired. Her limbic system had to decide if the error was a threat and it concluded that Alex was angry. Jane has a habit of thinking that people are out to get her, don't like her or are angry with her. She doesn't think about it. Her reactions happen almost instantly and unconsciously, even when the truth is that Alex was completely distracted and didn't even see her.

Changing habits, including emotional habits, is inherently uncomfortable. The Basal Ganglia are pulling one way, informing the brain and body that *this* is the way to respond, but in the effort to change a habit, we choose to do something else. The brain recognises that this is not right. Our body chemistry changes and sets up all kinds of error detections. This is one reason that change is hard; it is uncomfortable for the brain. Error detectors put the limbic system on full alert.

Putting the Brain Functions Together

The PFC focuses on a task, a goal or a project. That takes energy.

The Basal Ganglia take care of basic functions, like how to type or write, so that the PFC can focus on more important things, like problem solving. We might also have some other Basal Ganglia-supported habits, like drinking coffee or snacking while we work.

Meanwhile, the limbic system is monitoring all input, looking for ways to boost belonging, status, fairness, certainty and autonomy. At the same time, it is also constantly scanning the environment and is ready to react to potential threats. It is on the lookout for errors: changes to patterns, habits or even your own emotions, changes in others' behaviour – anything that shows up as different. When something out of the ordinary happens, the limbic system creates an alert with the intention of helping you survive.

> *For example: You're deeply focused on a project. You also have a slight annoyance about a disagreement you had yesterday with one of your colleagues. A bit of your energy goes to managing your emotions about that, so that you can focus on your project. An email gets your attention, and you learn that someone in the company has lost a contract. Since your PFC has been occupied a lot by your project and a little bit by that disagreement and you're tired, you don't have the PFC capacity to manage your limbic system at this moment, so you react and explode. Without thinking you "Reply All" to the email and criticise the "idiots" who messed up on that contract.*

> *It takes a good half hour to get focused again on the project. The chemicals – adrenaline and cortisol – shooting through your body make it nearly impossible to focus. But you force yourself to continue with your project, and you end up making a number of mistakes because really, your brain is not able focus on the details right now. You end up exhausted.*

With some basic knowledge of the limbic system, the PFC and the Basal Ganglia, let's turn our attention to the Sekhmed team and see how their brains have impacted their behaviour, before and after they have been through some leadership training and coaching.

56

Notes from Chapter 3

- Our limbic system is fine-tuned to help us survive; it rewards us if we do something "good" (that ensures survival) and helps us avoid perceived threats by generating a fear response.

- We have five times more circuitry for perceiving threats than rewards. A stimulus will most often be seen as a threat.

- The limbic triggers are: Belonging, Status, Fairness, Certainty and Autonomy.

- The Prefrontal Cortex (PFC) can manage our limbic system's reactions.

- The PFC is slow, lazy and weak but can be trained through awareness and mindfulness practices.

- Power can block mirror neurons and prevent a leader from focusing on people

- Multi-tasking is a myth.

- When something is different than usual, an error detector sends an alert which often turns into a fear response.

- The brain efficiently stores habits in the Basal Ganglia. This allows for quick responses without having to consult the slow PFC and think about what needs to be done.

4. Looking at the Team Through the Neuroscience Lens

We have had a look at what goes on in the individual brain. We talked about the PFC (prefrontal cortex), the Basal Ganglia and the limbic system with its error detection system and list of triggers. Now, let's have a look at what goes on with our team at Sekhmed through our neuroscience lens:

Kate, the Boss

How it Used to Be

Kate has excelled at moving up the corporate ladder, using her skills of creating relationships and accomplishing tasks. She is very status conscious and has made sure that her status has grown. She doesn't like it when her status is threatened, though she is usually able to control her reaction. She also likes control.

What Happened During the Last Six Months

At her leadership programme, Kate learned more about balancing task and relationship, and about influencing people. The impact was that the people who already had a good relationship with her felt closer. However, she also came back acting a bit different, and others felt threatened by that and immediately became more wary, their error detectors firing alerts because of her changes. Frank, for example, did not like that she started asking him more questions when she was trying to be more curious.

What's Really Going On

Kate has a life-long habit of seeking out status rewards. She's good at that. Her limbic system is constantly looking for threats to her status and independence. Her PFC is relatively well trained, and she monitors her actions to maintain good relationships. But she is a bit overworked and tired, and she's starting to become impatient. She's starting to lose some of her ability to "self manage," which is what George noticed when he entered her office. She was overwhelmed and unable to cover it up as usual.

Her challenge is to use her newly acquired skills of coaching. There isn't much context for this in her team, and the impact of her questioning style is such that she comes across as domineering and manipulating. Others get error detection from the fact that she's asking questions. They wonder what she's up to and start making some assumptions, which aren't all positive.

This then triggers limbic reactions. She gets frustrated and thinks to herself: *I'm not in control of my impact and I can't use these tools that I've learned. I've failed, and I'll stop using them.*

For the reader: Do you recognise people who are seeking status for themselves more than wanting to contribute to a team effort?

When have you given up trying something new because you didn't feel in control of what you were doing?

Cedric, the QA Manager

How It Used to Be

Cedric wants to belong. He has created habits of appeasing to make sure he doesn't get kicked out of the tribe. Stepping into his authority is hard for him; it's completely against his habitual way of being. So he tries to get people to do what he wants by being friendly. Unfortunately, that doesn't always work, and people find ways to ignore him.

What Happened During the Last Six Months

Cedric was working with a coach to improve his sense of authority and increase his self-esteem. People have a habit of ignoring Cedric, but most can see he has developed a sense of authority and power over the past few months. He's taken some risks, made more powerful statements and challenged a number of people to really look at their level of operating in terms of Quality Assurance. He can see a lot of problems, and he's risked his sense of belonging by pointing them out to people, which of course they don't like. On the other hand, many people respect the changes he's made in himself. They are the ones who recognise that as a whole, they are not abiding by any processes or procedures. Because of that, Cedric is making headway in implementing the QA standards. But in Maintenance, several influential people feel that quality is their turf, and they do not want to cooperate with him. Those people support one another and feel supported by their boss, and they become something of an anti-Cedric tribe. Their grouping together feels good to them, because they belong to a tribe with a purpose. None of this happened with intention, it just happened.

What's Really Going On

Lately, Cedric's PFC has supported him in letting go of his need to belong in order to do his job more effectively. It takes effort and a lot of energy to change this deep-seated habit, but he's making headway. His limbic system has been getting some status boosts – feel-good dopamine – from people who respect him, which helps balance the threats to belonging that he experiences. When there is pushback against him or his work, his limbic system and Basal Ganglia work together to try and reinstate his previous belonging habits. He will need to continue to use his PFC and choose to live through the discomfort while he changes his habits and behaviour. He gains more respect from some colleagues and this creates more belonging in the end, but it's hard for him to know that, in the midst of the discomfort of change.

As Cedric steps up, it creates reactions in others. Their error detectors fire off: Cedric isn't as "friendly," controllable or easy to manipulate as before. They start to have threat reactions, mostly in the form of fight or freeze. Maintenance people, in particular, have strong fight reactions because their sense of status and control is threatened. They naturally band together to create more of a sense of belonging, and this creates the anti-Cedric tribe.

For the reader: How does the need to belong and/or people pleasing prohibit honest dialogue in your organisation?

When do people band together against others in order to create a sense of belonging?

Frank, the Head of Maintenance

How It Used to Be

Frank is habituated to certainty, status and independence, and he's happy with that. He has less focus on belonging and fairness. He has long-term habits of being clear and direct – in military fashion – and people obey him. Often people feel safe around Frank because of the certainty he creates, so they generally obey. When people don't, Frank is in an uncomfortable place. Then, to create more stability and certainty, he tries harder to control, but that usually doesn't work so well either, as people resist that much control.

Frank doesn't want to take the leadership programme offered by Kate. He doesn't believe in "soft skills" and he sees himself as very effective, a motivator for his people and good at protecting his turf (and tribe). He believes he is a good leader and doesn't want to change anything in himself, but he certainly wants to change Iris, Paul, George and Cedric!

The status quo for Frank is feeling a sense of power. One of the downsides of this is that when experiencing power, the brain turns off empathy. This makes it difficult for Frank to read his colleagues' facial expressions or other indicators of mood. He can't feel their resistance or discomfort; he would have to be trained to start noticing them. It's possible, but it takes conscious effort.

What Happened During the Last Six Months

Frank still doesn't listen to Cedric, even though Cedric is being manlier. Frank notices the rebellion taking place in Maintenance, and he takes on the role as leader of the anti-Cedric pack. He starts to feel pressure from Paul and doesn't like it. Things are not getting better for him, and he blames these silly training programmes that people have been on. He's more on-guard than usual. He feels threatened by "the new winds blowing." He's tired of the extra effort he has to put in to remain cool and calm, and he's starting to lose his temper more often.

What's Really Going On

Frank's Basal Ganglia hold deeply ingrained habits of command and control. He's used to a sense of stability and confidence, which comes from status and control. His error detectors fire quickly when that stability is threatened. He's noticing changes, and of course that becomes uncomfortable. He's losing his cool demeanour because his limbic system is reacting to all the threats and his PFC, which works at keeping him cool, is getting maxed out and can't control it all anymore. When Frank reacts, he habitually goes for "fight," and this shows up as sarcasm and bullying. He does occasionally choose some "flight" responses, which show up as avoidance, for example, when he ignores Cedric. Frank's style of belonging is to be the alpha male, in the lead. He feels a sense of belonging and status when he leads the Maintenance guys who also refuse to follow Cedric. This helps him balance the needs of his limbic system after all that loss of control.

For the reader: Who are the people who don't notice their impact because power has a hold of them?

Who gains a sense of power by leading the rebels?

Iris, the Head of Sales

How It Used to Be

Iris wants to belong. Her lifelong habit is to be a people pleaser: give people what they want, and they will like you. The truth is that it's hurting her, but she doesn't have any idea how to do things differently. This is what feels right to her. She also wants to contribute and gain status, and that drives her to constantly improve her sales figures year after year. She is focused on the numbers with a kind of tunnel-vision, and when people don't appreciate and acknowledge her amazing sales figures, she tries harder and pushes her Sales team even more. She believes she is being helpful, looks for proof and finds it. Her brain is able to ignore any information that shows she's creating problems. She doesn't like Kate because Kate questions her, which threatens Iris's sense of belonging to the same tribe as Kate.

What Happened During the Last Six Months

The changes that Kate, Paul and Cedric have made don't really affect her. Her focus is on selling. She continues to see what she wants to see: more sales are better. She still longs to be recognised for selling more and for being a successful woman in a man's world. Kate's insistence that she's not being a team player makes no sense to her. Others' insistence that she's selling too many variants doesn't really make sense to her either. She thinks they don't know what's good for them and that they will see the light soon enough, but she's starting to show her irritation with them. Her desire to belong is actually backfiring.

What's Really Going On

Iris's Basal Ganglia hold habits of belonging, status and fairness. She feels threatened by Kate – another woman in management. Previously, she had the status of being the only woman in this man's world, and she doesn't like being bumped off her pedestal; it makes her even more determined to excel in sales.

She also feels threatened when people criticise her for selling too much. Her reaction is: *they are out to get me, so I'll just have to prove myself even more*, which is a vicious circle. Her focus is on what is working for her, and that blinds her to all other focus areas. It is hard for her to see her impact. It's possible that she suffers from the dynamic between power and empathy, with the power she's experiencing from her high sales figures shutting off her mirror neurons, so she cannot see what's happening for others. She can only see her numbers.

She gets a strong sense of belonging from her Sales team, with whom she has created a strong community (a silo) where they all feel safe together.

For the reader: Who are the people who keep doing more of the same, thinking it's the right thing, but don't understand that their efforts are also causing problems?

George, Head of Applications

How It Used to Be

George is a fire starter. He likes creating new projects. He started Sekhmed eight years ago and feels some sense of ownership of it, even though he technically sold the company and only agreed to stay on in order to ensure an effective transition over two years. After that, he agreed to stay on for another three years. He has invested in another new company, and his attention is often on that new startup. He still likes working at Sekhmed because he has a sense of belonging and a certain amount of status in the company.

He likes things to be fast paced. He wants to ignore the processes and procedures that are implemented as Sekhmed grows and becomes less entrepreneurial.

What Happened During the Last Six Months

George was getting more and more impatient and reactive. His fear was even telling him that he would be fired. But when Kate asked for help, he felt a boost of energy and perhaps power, and he was able to focus on the problems at hand rather than being defensive.

What's Really Going On

George gets doses of dopamine rewards for his status at the company, which make him feel good. He's a bit addicted to this and it's hard to give up. His brain is also attuned to the fast pace and mentality of startups, and anything that looks like too much organisation or corporate-ness creates error detections. His PFC is getting tired because he keeps trying to focus on too many things, and then it doesn't have much of a chance to manage his limbic reactions when they occur, so fear sometimes gets the best of him. Between more error detection and less filtering by the PFC, he becomes more reactive or fear-based in his behaviour. His form of reaction is to flee. He won't fight with Kate, Iris or the others, he just retreats to his office. Only with Paul, a fellow partner in distress, can he find a sense of belonging.

Kate's request for help reinstated some of his sense of power and status which seemed to balance his fears and allow him to focus better.

For the reader: When you have too many things on your plate, and you're trying to focus on too many things, do you recognise that you can easily become more reactive?

Consider some of the more reactive people in your workplace. Could their reactivity be a sign of being too tired and worn out, maybe from working too much, or even having personal challenges that occupy some of their brain?

Paul, Head of Platform

How It Used to Be

Paul wants to be seen, recognised and appreciated. He wants more status, although he also wants to belong. There seems to be an internal battle about, which is more important. He attached himself to George early on and was pleased that his efforts paid off when George suggested him for the lead of the Platform Group. He has all the time in the world for George and will pretty much side with him if the going gets tough.

What Happened During the Last Six Months

On his leadership course, Paul was excited to learn ways to increase his leadership skills. He returned to work feeling more powerful and confident, and he decided to try his new skills, even if he wasn't an expert yet. When his team ignored his ideas of the new responsibility matrix and role clarity, he got confused and frustrated and gave up. It was too hard to try to develop a new habit, and his old habits of people pleasing and needing to belong took over.

What's Really Going on

Paul's limbic system is looking for rewards of control and status. When his people ignore him, his error detectors fire off – that was not what he was expecting. Not only does he not get control and status rewards as he hoped he would, but he also gets a hit to certainty and control. So he flees; he gives up. He then reverts to his belonging-inspired habits, which are stored in his Basal Ganglia and will be enacted automatically if the PFC doesn't choose something else. He spends more time with George, often commiserating.

Paul's habits and his need for status and belonging that are met by his relationship with George, prevent him from being able to tell George "no" when he asks for unreasonable changes to the platform. This ends up causing problems down the road, but Paul's focus on belonging helps him to be blind to that impact.

For the reader: Are you familiar with those times when you have internal voices competing with one another? Might they be competing limbic needs?

How do limbic needs blind people to their impact?

Notes from Chapter 4

- Kate tries to be a superhero leader by fixing all the problems herself.

- When Cedric shows more power, the others are threatened by his new behaviours.

- Frank shows alpha male behaviours and mostly chooses to fight when threatened.

- Iris does what she's always done, expecting different results.

- George's typical reaction is to flee – avoid the problem.

- Paul tries something new; it isn't perfect right away, so he quickly reverts to old habits.

5. What To Do About It?

Knowing about the brain helps us understand some of the common ills of today's typical workplace, where people are often driven by self-interest and find it hard to work in teams; where competition, silo mentality, revenge, suspicion and refusal to cooperate are common daily experiences. These are much more easily understood when we see that they are largely driven by our survival-focused limbic system.

We seem to have so much working against us. Well, possibly we do, but we also have a great capacity to do things differently. The brain has a tremendous capacity for clarity, collaboration, creativity and compassion. We just need to focus on the latter instead of the former. Perhaps that's easier said than done, but we can learn to overcome our reactive nature and leverage our strengths instead.

Recovering From Reactions and Using the PFC

Neuroscientists tell us there are a few ways to recover from reactions.

The simplest way is called **labelling**. This is about recognizing how we're feeling, perhaps just stating to ourselves, or out loud: "I'm angry," "I'm reacting," "I'm upset," "I notice I am…." It's about noticing one's reactions. That in itself often reduces the reaction.

A slightly more sophisticated form of recovery is to **reappraise**. Reappraising is a matter of seeing the situation differently. Jane can realise that Alex is having a rough time of things at the moment, and instead of being upset that he didn't say "Good morning," she could have compassion. And just that change of mind will change her reaction.

Neuroscientists show that **mindfulness practice** – a form of meditation – can strengthen and grow the PFC. Stronger PFCs have more capacity to manage limbic reactions and more capacity to focus for longer periods of time. With more PFC capacity, we get more of all the things listed in chapter 3: focus, goal setting, discipline, compassion, etc.

Mindfulness is a practice of non-judgemental awareness. It's a matter of just noticing what's going on without deciding if something is good or bad, or right or wrong. Mindfulness can be practised for ten minutes or thirty minutes a day. People who do so are notably more calm, cool and collected. Mindfulness can also be used in a moment to defuse a situation and see what's going on more clearly.

Someday, it will probably be normal to have meditation rooms in companies. It may sound far-fetched in 2014, but research reveals that mindfulness has a tremendous positive impact on the brain and therefore a positive impact on people, their interactions and working cultures.

Creating New Habits

We can learn to change habits, but it takes time and attention. If we want to stop responding habitually with anger, for example, we need to first recognise that we're angry – we need to catch ourselves reacting with anger. Then we need to train ourselves to respond in a different way. This takes conscious awareness, attention and choice. It is possible, but it does take effort and our attention. If we're too busy focusing on a hundred other things, we might not have the conscious capacity to make the change. So we need to give ourselves a little bit of space and time.

Building new habits requires repetition and practice. That practice can happen in a "real" situation, but also in a practice situation. The brain doesn't know the difference between imagination and "reality," so practise, practise, practise in whatever situation you can – even if it's made up. Practise a new desired habit over and over and it will stick.

We can create habits of curiosity rather than defensiveness, or of compassion rather than blame. The recovery techniques in the previous section can also become habits. It's all a matter of what we practise and reinforce every day.

Summary

The human brain is a remarkable instrument. It is a complicated and massively interconnected mix of animal limbic system, sophisticated prefrontal cortex (PFC), a set of Basal Ganglia which store automatic habits, and a number of other significant brain regions.

Unfortunately, we often unconsciously allow our limbic system to run our lives because it's faster, easier and more efficient. It's also automatic. This underuse of the PFC and over-reliance of the limbic system has us create fear-based environments, which lead to breakdown of communication, trust and collaboration.

It's so easy to create and sustain a fear-based culture. But it's also possible to create and maintain a more positive and nurturing culture if we choose to do so. It would mean learning to reduce our fear-based reactions and increase our PFC's ability to stay in charge. It would require us to create nurturing habits rather than destructive ones.

Leaders of organisations can start by reducing reaction-creating stimuli. This might mean being more forthcoming about upcoming changes in order to create more certainty for individuals. It might mean making sure people get acknowledged and recognised regularly. Leaders can make sure people get treated fairly, and so on.

But it's not just up to the leaders to control the whole environment. Everyone could benefit from understanding the brain and learning to recover from reactions, have compassion for others' reactions and reduce the reactions they cause in others. All members of an organisation could be encouraged to train their PFCs, so they can be more engaged and have better focus and awareness.

If we can do that, we could start to make changes together.

If we were to strengthen our PFCs, our improved focus would allow us to get more done in a shorter period of time. We could be more compassionate with our colleagues when they react and prevent ourselves from reacting in kind, thus sparing ourselves the ongoing reactions we would then waste energy having to recover from.

With fully functioning PFCs, we would be able to manage our fears of each other, and instead we could choose to focus on each other's brilliance. We could overcome our individualistic and competitive tendencies and truly trust others. From there, we could share ideas and co-create together. We would be able to share ideas without fear of ridicule, so we would increase our ability to create and innovate. We would not waste time on petty grievances, but instead we would be able to work through conflicts in a calmer manner.

It may sound too good to be true, but the capacity is right there in our brains, ready for us to tap into.

Notes from Chapter 5

- When we notice a limbic reaction, we can use techniques to recover:

  Labelling
  Reappraisal
  Mindfulness practice

- We can create new habits, but it takes repetition, practice and time.

PART 3
Systems Thinking

6. Introduction to Our Social Brains

As we described in the previous chapter, the human brain is a social brain; a lot of our brain's circuitry is focused on how we are in relationship with others. It's as if we were designed to live and work in families, clans and teams. In this chapter, we move to a systemic view of teams, business and in particular of Sekhmed.

Humans Exist in Tribes

In the early days, tribes were collections of families, and their purpose was for the families to exist and thrive together to support and protect one another. Today, we still form tribes in all kinds of ways, at all levels of society: there are the Presidents Clubs for presidents of organisations; there are the ladies who lunch; there are street gangs whose members often don't have strong families and need some kind of group to belong to. It happens naturally – we flock. Maybe we flock together because we have similar ideas or ideals. Maybe we flock together for survival or perceived survival. Maybe we flock together to create something, and then develop similar ideals as a result of having a collective purpose.

Tribes and Roles

There are usually many roles and functions within a tribe. In the ancient tribes, there were hunters and gatherers. There were fire keepers, storytellers, warriors, lookouts, protectors, nurturers, child carers, musicians, leaders and wise elders. This is still true today in our societies and in our companies. Not everyone does everything. There is a collective effort. We are all taken care of by the collective contributions of society. This is the setting in which our brains evolved and how we're used to operating. Tribes, teams, departments and companies all need to cooperate in order to be successful. They need to work as a system for the good of the whole. Unfortunately, they aren't always successful at doing this.

Individualism Versus Collectivism

We need tribes, but we also have a need for individualism. As we saw in the last chapter, there's a pull between our need to belong and our need for status within a group. We have a limbic system that points us to belonging, but our needs for autonomy and status – relative to others – might pull us away from belonging. This translates to a tug of war between being a tribe member and being an individualist. It seems we were designed to balance the two. But sometimes we get hung up on one of these to the exclusion of the other. A hang up on either one can pose problems.

We are aware that different cultures (national, family, religious, etc.) often encourage us one way or another. Western cultures tend to be more individualistic, while Eastern cultures tend to be more collectivistic: individuals only know themselves because of the groups they are a part of. Each of us has the potential for both. How we are raised will create habits of social behaviour.

As we stated at the very beginning of this book, we are raised to do our schoolwork as individuals, we are graded separate from others and in many cases school is inherently competitive. We are often asked to consider: *What do I want to be when I grow up? What are my values? Who am I? What are my skills and my strengths?*

Then we get a job with a salary based on our previous individual achievements and possibly a bonus that will be based each year on our individual performance.

Then we're put on a team. And that can be confusing and confronting.

In the previous chapter, we talked about how the brain will quickly develop habits for the sake of efficiency. When habits are reinforced, they become stronger. If a child has been taught his whole life to think as an individual, by the time he is an adult, he will have developed some strong habits of thinking about his own survival: me versus the others. The Basal Ganglia have stored the "me first" mentality; it's all about me. Fortunately, those are just habits and they can be changed, but we need to understand the strength of habits and influence from the larger culture.

We need to understand that we have to train ourselves to think in terms of a team, division or company. It takes time and training to change such strong habits. We might just need to teach people about what it means to think TEAM instead of thinking ME.

Individual Leadership

Our Western view of leadership has also been very individualistic. We have a strong preference for the leader as hero; the great and powerful CEO that comes in and saves the company. Leadership programmes are also usually individualistic. We send the individual out to a programme and hope that he or she will come back as a better leader and improve the team's or company's performance.

Leadership development is frequently about how an individual leader can have influence on a team or on colleagues, and about how to be more powerful, influential and visionary. This approach often fails to work because it just doesn't consider the rest of the organisation.

Coaching too is inherently individualistic. Individual coaching is, well, about the individual. There are myriad styles of coaching, but we think it's safe to say that it's usually about the individual: about his or her style, desired impact and influence, individual dreams, goals, strengths, and much of it without the context of the organisation.

We trust a body of work done by George Binney et al at the Ashridge Business School in the UK, which is described in their book, Living Leadership. Their research shows us that the "superhero" model of leadership isn't working. Leaders need to pay attention to the teams they work for or serve; they need to pay attention to the culture in which they work and how to tap into the collective potential of diverse human systems. We enjoy their definition of leadership:

"Leadership is not about knowing the answer; it is the capacity to release the collective intelligence and insight of groups and organisations."

Culture Is Powerful

Let's discuss culture in general. The definition of culture is the ideas, customs, and social behaviour of a particular people or society. Culture is "how we do things around here," and also how we think: what's important, what's sacred and what's not.

As soon as a group of people gather, the seeds of the culture are planted. They grow and deepen as the group matures. We become accustomed to one another. Over time, habits are embedded. Our brains see that those habits are the one and only way things are to be done. Then, according to our limbic systems, it's much safer to keep doing what we've been doing. Anything else (change!) is a threat, or too much effort to think about. Error detectors are activated in many brains at once if we try to do things differently. It's so easy to create habits of how we do things, but it is difficult to change them.

Companies have cultures. These cultures have their own characteristics around being process oriented, creative, aggressive, masculine or feminine. While the whole company has a culture, so does each of the teams and departments within it. There is a culture for the whole system and there are cultures for each of the sub-systems.

Trying to change ingrained habits can be quite difficult because each individual has to change habits, and we already know that takes energy and focus. And that's another thing that's difficult about change initiatives: We have Basal Ganglia-embedded habits, and it's really hard to change those.

No matter where or how a culture began, the individuals in that culture will adapt one way or another, and now we have a collection of habits, ways we interact and perhaps beliefs we buy into together. We can then create an identity based on those: *We are the people who sell. We are the team that hunts buffalo. We are the fast moving, get-it-done quickly team. We are the team that doesn't like that other team, and so on.*

Imagine joining a company that's all about adaptability and fast pace. It's successful and grows. It has to create processes, and eventually it becomes bureaucratic and weighed down by procedures. The whole culture has to change and that means that each of the individuals in it also has to change. Sometimes they don't or won't, and so they leave. This happens all the time with companies as they grow. Company growth requires changing the culture and that requires the individuals to change their habits. We need to admit that it just isn't that easy.

Mergers and acquisitions create culture clashes. There are so many mergers that fail because the cultures just could not integrate.

Some cultures are toxic. Perhaps blame and criticism are the norm, or contempt and sarcasm may run rampant throughout the system. Those too can be difficult to change.

A Simple Model for Change

We'd like to describe the Edge Model, which is a very simple model that we use to describe change. It helps us understand what's happening when change is afoot.

The Edge Model was first illustrated by Arnold Mindell, and its use in systems work was expanded by Marita Fridjhon and Faith Fuller in the Organization and Relationship Systems Coaching (ORSC™) approach by CRR Global. CRR Global and the ORSC model also inspire much of our thinking about systems.

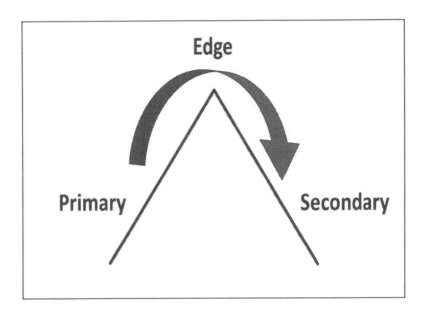

The model might be simple, but it paints a powerful picture for people. The Primary side is where we are now, how we identify ourselves or how we do things currently. The Secondary side contains all the unknown possibilities of how we could be or could do things – perhaps a desired state or a sense of what we need to become in the future. To get from where we are now (a primary), to something new (a secondary), we have to cross the edge. Some edges are easy, like shifting from a meeting to being back at our desk. Some edges are huge, like facing retirement. Edges are individual and there are collective edges as well. When a company identifies itself as a small startup, and then sees signs that it is getting bigger and needs more processes and procedures, the company is at an edge. When a team or any system is at an edge, then everyone in that system is also brought to an edge.

Secondaries are unlimited: there are infinite possibilities of who we could be, or what could happen next, and all of them are on the other side of the edge. It's as if we cannot quite see those options. When we go to make a change, we have to move from our known place over the edge to the unknown. As we know from neuroscience, the unknown is not comfortable. The brain doesn't like it. Crossing the edge can be quite difficult. A lot of things can happen at the edge, for example: excitement, resistance, reactions, drama and toxic behaviour. All those behaviours are indications that the individuals and the system as a whole are at an edge. We call those *Edge Behaviours.*

It's useful to know about edge behaviours because when we see those behaviours, we can see them simply as behaviours that indicate that a person or a system is at an edge. Then we can get curious about the edge itself.

Examples of Edges:

John has worked as a mechanic for twenty years. Now, his company wants him to work in Sales, because he has always been good with the customers. The salary is better and all other aspects seem like a good thing from the outside. But John has to change his identity. It's a big edge for him.

From psychology, we learn that some of the biggest stressors in life are death, marriage, divorce and having children. These are big edges.

Smaller edges might be: moving to a new office (you have to learn to get there a different way), switching to a new car, getting a new computer.

In order to navigate an edge, you need to engage your PFC and consciously focus until you make new habits. It takes brainpower. When that's happening, it's not easy to focus on other goals, stick to your diet or change other things, and it's not as easy to manage the limbic system and limbic reactions.

A system, team or company will come to an edge with events such as a change in ownership, a reorganisation, taking on a big new project, implementing new policies, hiring a number of new employees or downsizing. There can be widespread edge behaviour. There might be enthusiasm, bursts of creativity, chaos, more productivity or a quick shift followed by a rapid downturn in productivity. There might be a strike or other kinds of revenge. There might be resistance and complaints. There might be sadness at the loss of other colleagues or fear that one's job is going to be cut next. We must recognise that all of these are human events that we need to take the time to adapt to.

Often at a time of change, some of the individuals in the organisation make the shift and others don't. This is a great time for silos or tribes to form: perhaps the ones who go with the change and the ones who don't. Each group sticks together because there is comfort in belonging. There can be a lot of strife between these different tribes. It's so easy to believe we're right and they're wrong.

If leaders publically praise the ones who embrace the change, they will probably create status rewards in that group while creating a revenge impulse in the people who don't embrace the change. This just adds fuel to the fire.

But the people who resist are just at an edge, together. Their limbic systems don't like change or the unknown. The people might not understand what is happening, or why. They might collectively feel threats to status; perhaps they don't know what will happen to their jobs. Maybe their survival really is at stake, or maybe their limbic systems just imagined those threats. They band together for comfort and then reinforce their beliefs together, which only makes the reactions stronger.

It gets complicated quite quickly when we get all those limbic systems together. In the name of survival, people react to change and then there are reactions to reactions and on and on it goes, possibly spinning out of control.

It isn't always drastic. Small changes are happening all the time. Edge behaviours are happening all the time. Sometimes the edges are all eventually crossed and sometimes people get stuck and the problems grow.

Let's see if we can make all of this more practical by looking at Sekhmed through the lenses of systems thinking and the social brain.

Notes from Chapter 6:

- It's natural for humans to exist in tribes and natural for different people to take on different roles in the tribe.

- Culture is simply "how we do things around here."

- Any change in culture is a change and will lead to "edge behaviour."

- The Edge Model helps us understand that change is just an edge to cross.

- When an individual or a team confronts an edge, i.e., is up against a change, it often creates behaviours that might not be useful in actually making the change.

- Most edge behaviours are fear-based.

7. Looking at the Team Through the Systemic Lens

With the above discussion of tribes, roles, individualism versus collectivism, identity and culture, and the Edge Model in mind, let's look at Sekhmed and see what new insights we find.

Identity, Culture and Edges

Sekhmed is a relatively young organisation. Most of the people identify with being part of a startup, but it's changed so much in its eight years that they don't really know what it is anymore. *Are we a small startup or a larger organisation? Are we our own company, or do we belong to the Corporation?* Mostly they think of themselves as an independent startup, but there is some doubt about that.

Most of the people have habits of operating in a way that small organisations can pull off: being flexible, adaptable, quick to respond, and with direct relationships between programmers and customers, among other things. However, they're getting a little too big to do so, and not all the parts of the system have caught up to that.

The founder of the original company and software system is still working in the company, along with a number of his original colleagues. They think of themselves as a fast-paced organisation and want to continue to be a part of a startup. That is their mindset. There's nothing wrong with a startup mindset, but it's getting in the way of the organisation growing into something larger and more stable.

So the Sekhmed division as a whole is at an edge with its identity. The mere fact that Kate was brought on to shift the organisation into a different mindset could put them at an edge. The fact that Cedric was sent in with a formal Quality Assurance approach could send them to an edge. *QA? That's for old, sedate companies!* Do you see the identity problem they have? When a system is at an edge, the individuals within it will experience edges at different times and in different magnitude. And as individuals experience things differently, it can create wedges between them.

The Sekhmed culture is also a right/wrong culture. If things aren't working, something must be wrong and someone is to blame. Finger pointing is a commonly accepted practice. Isolating the problem and trying to fix it has been an approach used for a long time.

Tribes

The Sekhmed division has one common purpose: it is one big tribe dedicated to a single software package with variable applications. The departments within this division have different functions: Sales, software development (Platform and Applications) and Maintenance. Each of those departments has a different culture. The people who work in the Applications department are a little more adventurous and fast paced than the people who work in the Platform department. This makes sense as the platform is intended to be the stable part of the software, while applications are smaller and they shift and change. Maintenance is more meticulous and concerned with fixes and long-term stability of the package.

Even teams within the departments have slightly different cultures. Within the Platform department, one of the teams was open to the idea of quality assurance procedures, and the others were not. They were willing to think differently and to work differently. This difference created a rift.

In Sekhmed, the various departments have forgotten that they all work for one organisation and one purpose, that there is one software package that they collectively work on. And they are completely disconnected from the Corporation that owns them, so much so that most of them are ready to get rid of the Corporation representative, Cedric.

They have fallen into silo thinking by creating tribes, which are in opposition to other tribes. Sales is its own tribe, thinking that its function is to bring in the money. Maintenance has a very strong identity and sense of tribe: Us against Them. They don't think of themselves as part of Sales or of Sales as part of Maintenance. But shouldn't they be? They're all working for the same company and the same overall purpose.

Roles

As the company, or division grew, more roles were required. At the beginning, everybody did everything that was needed. There were no dedicated Maintenance people, and especially not a person fully dedicated to QA. For the first few years, George, the creator of Sekhmed, worked on both software development and maintenance. Over time, roles expanded but weren't always well defined. This created confusion for a lot of people.

After their leadership courses, both Kate and Paul wanted to work on role clarity. It was sorely needed and could make a huge difference in how the organisation operated. But there was a lot of resistance, because people felt micro-managed. It would have helped them cross that particular edge if role clarity had been introduced in a slightly different way: if people had some choice in how it was created, if they were recognised and appreciated along the way, if there was more certainty about why this was being done.

Then there's what we call internal roles. Frank is a strong character and thinks of himself as a leader. He doesn't have the title of division head, but he has an internal role of leader. People listen to him, and he is used to people listening to him. He is at an edge when someone doesn't listen to him.

What is the role of Maintenance? And QA? Are they separate? Should Maintenance hold the QA role? How do these roles relate?

When the Customer Service team was moved from Maintenance to the Sales group, did that change their identity and/or role? It certainly changed some relationships and created some disturbance. What was their function overall? If management had looked at it in that way, they might not have moved the Customer Service team to a different group. Or if they had created more certainty for everyone when doing so, perhaps the shift would have been easier.

Individualism and Collectivism

How does individualism show up on this team? Many of our characters are interested mostly in their own self-preservation: in keeping their own jobs, in looking good, in having an influence over others. Iris is interested in sales and being the star at creating contracts and revenue. She's not looking at the whole system and what it needs. She's concerned about numbers and her status. She might also be concerned about bonuses for herself and her team members. This kind of reward can skew how sales are made. It might look reckless from others' perspectives.

Frank is also quite individualistic. He thinks that he alone can save the company, if only everyone listens to him and does things his way. George is more concerned about his original desires for the company he created than he is for its evolution and current needs.

The leadership programme that Kate went on empowered her as an individual. She came back with some good ideas, but it's up to her to try to implement them throughout the division. The same goes for Paul. Cedric too: in getting coached, he found his personal power. Even though he likes to make sure a team is getting along, he puts his own personal need for comfort ahead of the need for honesty and truth and occasional conflict.

All three of them benefitted from doing the coaching and the programmes, yet there is something that doesn't quite work in the implementation of what they learned.

Collectivism is happening in some of the different departments. Sales is a team that works well together, for example, as they're on a mission together. They have a culture of "Sell, sell, sell; encourage customers to buy special functions and variants. We can do it!" The Maintenance group is also a strong "We" culture. Maintenance and Customer Service felt like they belonged together and were quite upset when separated.

On the level of the executive team, however, individualism rules, and that has an impact throughout the organisation.

Kate herself is individualistic. She has taken the burden upon herself to find solutions to all the problems. It is her individualistic mindset that sends people on different programmes and doesn't create a wider culture change programme. But of course, that's what she has learned her whole life. For her to act differently would require a big change within her.

The Systemic Habits – the Culture of the Organisation

The systematic habits, or culture of the organisation, won't shift just by sending a few individuals on a programme or getting them individual coaching. We've seen that a few of the changes that were needed took place, but when we change one part of a formed system, it rocks the balance.

Picture a hanging mobile with a few arms and various objects dangling from it. It finds its place of balance and stability. Then imagine taking one of the small pieces from the middle and changing its weight, shape or size. When put back, it causes the rest of the mobile to shift and move before it can rebalance itself.

That's our image of what happens if you train a part of the system on people skills without letting the rest of the system know about it. The individual comes back and starts having a different impact on others. That shakes things up and moves things around. It forces people to an edge and leaders then get surprised and frustrated when their colleagues "resist" the change.

The culture needs to be addressed as a whole.

Edge Behaviour

There is edge behaviour all over the place in Sekhmed. The blame, discord and conflicts are just indications that the system is at an edge or facing many edges.

We can see that the edge of shifting from a smaller, fast-paced organisation to a bigger organisation creates a number of edge behaviours. All the drama about Cedric isn't about Cedric himself. It's edge behaviour about having to do things differently. Cedric is a representative of that edge and many people focus on him as the problem. True, he could probably do his job better, but forcing one person to implement such a change without widespread buy-in is just a recipe for disaster and an invitation for a lot of edge behaviour and potential conflict.

Introducing changes, as Paul tried to do in creating a roles and responsibility matrix, created such strong edge behaviour from his team that it made it impossible to cross that edge.

The finger-pointing at Sales and their heel digging is also edge behaviour indicating that something needs to be addressed. Maybe we can't see yet what that edge is, but the edge behaviour gives us a place to start looking. Edge behaviours give us opportunities to find out what's really going on in a system. Often we try to fix or squash those behaviours or fire people who have those behaviours, and in so doing, we miss the opportunity to learn what's going on.

Notes from Chapter 7

- The whole leadership team considers their Roles and how they are all at different Edges.

- The Sekhmed culture includes habits they developed when they were a startup. These are beginning to create problems.

- Rival tribes have formed around various issues.

- Roles are not being held well.

- Individualism and self-protection tend to keep the team from working in harmony.

- Edge behaviour is happening a lot: finger pointing, resistance, resentment.

- If we look at the behaviours as stress signals, we might be able to get curious about the stress and address it at that level rather than trying to squash the behaviours themselves.

8. What To Do About It?

Being armed with information about systems helps us have a broader view of what's going on. We look at the organisation and all the dynamics in it as a whole system. What is the nature of this system? What is the culture? What are the habits and norms? What is the system trying to tell us? How toxic is it? What roles are unclear or unoccupied? What are the edge behaviours, the signals of distress that are trying to tell us something?

Instead of trying to fix this problem and that conflict, we take it all together as one big picture and work with everyone to help them see themselves as one big entity with a number of symptoms.

From that view, the organisations can often see for themselves what they need to shift in order to create a more harmonious working environment and to make the changes together. So the first step is to create some understanding about what a system is and have them view themselves as a whole system.

Perhaps they most need to clarify collective goals. "We, as a company, are growing; we need to move from a fast moving startup to have more processes and procedures. That might not be as fun, but this is where we are now. How can we do that together? And together we figure out how to work with quality assurance. Together we decide what should be sold to the customers and what is too much." When those decisions are made together, there will be much more buy-in and much less tribal warfare.

There might be some need for training. We can train people to deal with conflict, clarify roles, pay attention to edge behaviour, and work with it rather than try to stamp it out. We can train them in communication skills to help smooth some of the toxic edge behaviours. We can help systems to consciously and intentionally create the culture they want. We can help them create safety, mostly by understanding the brain's reactivity, so that individuals don't have to worry so much about their own survival and instead can be more team-oriented rather than self-oriented.

But it's helpful to do all of that training within the context of systemic change: Personal change for the sake of the whole.

Summary

We have social brains. Humans exist in tribes, groups, families and societies. Each tribe or society develops a culture which strongly influences how things get done and how members think. A business is a type of society complete with a culture comprising a whole lot of "How we do things around here" rules – written and unwritten. That culture is powerful and contains a lot of energy and inertia. There are a lot of brains involved, a lot of Basal Ganglia that know how to do things "right," and when those get together, they create a strong force that is largely resistant to change.

Trying to shift a culture is like trying to move a river. It's not easy to shift the direction of a stream or current.

As humans, we naturally vacillate between focusing on belonging to a tribe and focusing on our own personal success, self-preservation or relevance within the tribe. We are often trained in our early years to be either more individualistic, focusing on our own self-preservation, or more collectivistic, focussing on the benefit of the whole.

When a lot of people focus primarily on their own self-preservation, it often isn't helpful to the larger collective (team or company); in fact, it can be quite detrimental to the whole. Unfortunately, there are so many ways that businesses encourage individualism: most bonus schemes are based on individual performance; salaries are individual; feedback is usually individual; and problems are often considered an individual's problem. "Difficult" individuals are treated as individual problems.

We need to find ways to point people's attention back to the whole. They will probably only do that if they know their personal survival is secure. Security and safety become key.

We need to learn to take care of our system and how we behave in it. We tend to take self-care seriously; what if we took team-care just as seriously? It's worth taking some time to pay attention to how we are behaving together and how we could be even better.

If we want teams that collaborate better, we need to address individuals' sense of safety. We need to look at how we treat one another, how we support one another and how we come together as a team. We need to keep each other's limbic systems in mind. How can we create rewards in each other rather than reactions?

If we really want to create and innovate together, there needs to be enough safety to propose new ideas without fear of ridicule or being thrown out of the tribe. There needs to be trust. The team needs to be able to be critical of ideas and for team members not to take it personally.

So let's take care of our tribes and teams.

In our experience, when we have seen teams of people make a shift to being more team-focused, it becomes a self-perpetuating positive cycle because:

- A well-functioning team creates a more enjoyable place to work

- People perform better when they're happier

- People focus more on the team and they appreciate the team more, which reinforces the positivity

- People feel emotionally safe and sufficiently well taken care of, so they quickly learn to "lean in" to the team and share resources more

- When brains are not having to react or quell reactions, there's more capacity to focus, think and find ways to be creative.

Notes from Chapter 8

- Look at the big picture, the tribe, the system and the roles.

- Create enough safety for everybody involved. Culture change requires individuals to cross their own edges and they will need to feel safe enough to make those shifts.

PART 4
Using What We Know

9. The Overall Approach

We have integrated neuroscience and systems thinking in our approach to facilitating change in organisations. We use experiential learning methods in training and coaching formats. This chapter presents how we do this.

First we look at the system as a whole: What are the outcomes or changes that the organisation wants? What is the leadership style they want? What is the culture they want? What are the behaviours and habits that need to be created and embedded in that culture? Where are the problem areas, and what aspects of the culture might be creating them? We work with the organisation to develop some criteria or objectives for the changes they want to make. Organisations often want less strife, a more effective working environment and more collaboration and innovation. That is our focus in this description.

Leadership development and culture change need to happen together for any change to be successfully implemented in the organisation. If you are trying to change a culture, you need to start with the leaders, and that means some form of leadership development. If the leaders are not involved, it is unlikely that culture change will happen. On the other hand, if you want to develop leaders, we know that it cannot be done in a vacuum because if leaders change their approach to leading, the people they lead will need to understand those differences and changes, so that they can follow well with minimal reaction. That becomes a type of culture change. So whether culture or leadership is the focus for change, the other is required as well.

In our approach to change, we start with leadership development.

We highly recommend that leadership development happen in-house. We've seen too many examples where leaders learn something in an external programme and then try to bring it back to their workplace. But the tools they've learned seem foreign, they don't belong to the company culture and the leaders feel pushback. The leaders haven't learned how to implement the tools or how to tell others what they're doing and why. Training in-house creates one common language and approach to leadership that the leaders can then work on implementing together. If they have agreements together about how they will try new tools and approaches, they can support one another and they can train the rest of the organisation about the approach. It's one less hurdle to get over if they learn together.

In-house also allows leaders to learn and grow together. Not only does learning together create a much better chance of implementing their new learning, they also get to know one another better and create a positive sense of belonging. Incredible bonds are created when people learn together. That will serve the organisation well.

After leadership development, practice and support for the changes are needed. Part of that will be in supporting the leaders and part in supporting the rest of the organisation.

Leaders can be supported in their individual shifts with coaching or other approaches. Team coaching is important to help them make the changes together in how they interact with one another.

It is also necessary to train the people who work for those leaders in how to respond to this new leadership style. If leaders are trying to empower their team members, for example, the team members need to know that and understand how to respond. That is the only way the leadership training will really be implemented successfully. Otherwise it's a waste of time and money.

In the next few chapters, we go into more detail about how we implement the various elements of our change process. We will look at:

- Leadership development – what the leaders need to know about the brain and about "the people system"

- How to train and learn – explaining the experiential method

- Coaching as a support mechanism.

Notes from Chapter 9

- Look at the system as a whole.

- Leadership development and culture development need to happen together because you can't have one without the other.

- Train people in-house, together.

- Changes need to be supported over time.

- Change takes time.

10. Leadership Development

Leadership development starts with training and creating awareness about the nature of leadership.

Leadership happens in relationship. The model of the superhero leader belongs to a bygone era. As leaders, we now need to respect people, grow them and allow them to make mistakes. First, we need to learn more about ourselves and understand the environment that we create. Then we need to figure out how to create safety and positivity and how to grow people. We need to understand people and behaviour, and a bit of brain science goes a long way. We include the following elements in our leadership development programmes for this purpose.

Understanding the Basics of Human Behaviour and the Brain:

We highlight below some of what we covered in the neuroscience section of this book.

Reactions

Leaders themselves need to grow their own emotional understanding and self-control, learn about their own reactions and recovery. One of the biggest complaints in organisations is that leaders are abusive and do not walk their talk.

So start with yourself. Learn what drives your own behaviour. This sounds very simple, but it's not. We each have a lifetime of habits and behaviours. We react to various stimuli. We interpret all kinds of events as threats. The training for leaders to understand what's going on might only take a day or two, but the work to implement it could take a lifetime. This kind of training definitely needs to be followed up with a support system for individuals. It could be in the form of groups that get together and support one another in not reacting, a programme outside work that helps individuals manage their emotions, or working with a coach. Whatever it is, there is individual work to do so that leaders can best create positive human interactions with others and with the teams they are a part of.

Recovery

The recovery elements of labelling, reappraisal and non-judgemental awareness, or mindfulness, are essential, and they need to be practised. It will never be enough just to teach people these concepts: they need to be given the opportunity to experience their reactions, and then to recover by using these recovery techniques. React, recover, react, recover, etc. Most people will have some very strong neural pathways of reaction. The training and all subsequent support and coaching can help them create new neural pathways, and strengthen those pathways of recovery.

A specific tip: Don't give feedback to someone when you or they are in the middle of a reaction. It will only create other reactions and quite possibly long term revenge. Recover first, and then come back to the feedback.

Reducing Reactions in Others

Everyone, and especially leaders, can benefit from learning about what creates reactions in others and the impact our own behaviour has on them. Understanding normal human reactions can help us learn how to lead and how to enact changes in organisations.

Leaders need to create as much safety as possible to reduce reactive behaviour. Teaching everyone in an organisation about reactive behaviour and to understand their own reactive nature, and supporting them to manage those reactions, would be hugely beneficial.

People need certainty, so when creating change, create as much certainty as possible. Ask for input from others in order to give them a chance to belong and to raise their own status. They can have autonomy and independence if they are engaged in shaping a vision and feel responsible for making it real. If people are told what to do, however, they are more likely to resist. Then they'll find others who agree with them, create a tribe, and we'll end up with rival factions or rebelling tribes.

In general, reduce the threats to the limbic triggers: Be as fair as possible. Create certainty. Allow employees to have some amount of independence, choice and autonomy. Encourage belonging and take care when moving people from one group to another. And make sure people's status isn't threatened.

Personal Development Is Normal

Leaders need to get over their fear of "soft skills." For one thing, they're no longer soft: This is hard science we're talking about here. Our behaviours directly create behaviours in others. Leaders need to learn to notice the reactions that arise in response to their actions. Leaders can learn to appreciate, acknowledge, complement and praise people in a way that works. They can learn to create safe and positive environments. All of that learning begins with their own personal development: awareness of themselves and their own reactions, managing those reactions, and taking responsibility for the impact they have on others.

Positivity

Research shows that there is a strong link between positivity and productivity. Leaders who create a positive atmosphere and help their teams to maintain one will be helping their teams to become more productive, creative, innovative and happy. Happy people stay and collaborate better with others.

This isn't about removing conflict but about learning how to have *productive* conflict. Teach people and teams to work through conflict rather than suppress it. Allow it. Know that reactions happen. Allow people to be reactive from time to time. Teach your people to recover from their own reactions and to self-manage in the face of others' reactions. Normalise reactions. Normalise recovery and personal development.

An important part of creating more positivity is to remove toxic behaviours. Toxic behaviours (for example, blame, criticism and contempt) can be deeply embedded, so there need to be opportunities for people to experience doing things differently together. Of course there is individual learning to be done for people who are particularly addicted to contempt, rage or defensiveness, but learning to behave differently together and to hold a whole team accountable for a different style of behaviour will help them in the implementation of the new way.

Creating Safety

We could say that first and foremost, a leader's job is to create safety, to create an environment where people can learn and want to learn. That will *only happen* if there is safety to make mistakes and learn from them. Why learning? Because if people only do what they've done before, they're acting like robots. Most of the time, workers are learning to do something new, figuring out new ways of doing something or adapting to some kind of change. That's all learning, and learning requires safety.

When people experience something they interpret as a threat, they will respond with a fear reaction. If people are always watching out for their safety and security, it forces them into an individual, protective frame of mind.

Therefore, understanding how to reduce reactions in the people we lead is important. If we're always creating threats, people will always be in fear. It's easy to create threats. Every change we make can elicit a fear response. So create certainty for people. Allow them to be in control of their work as much as possible.

Some Systems Dynamics

It is also important for people to understand some key elements about our social brains. Firstly, that the pull to create tribes is powerful. People will rally together around positive intentions or negative ones. Give them reasons to come together around the positive and around what's possible: *We are the team that creates great designs together.* Acknowledge teams together, rather than celebrating individuals. The leader needs to notice the destructive or "toxic" behaviours in a system and know that they are a systemic dynamic, not just the fault of one or more individuals.

Another well-known systemic dynamic that is highly useful to be aware of is the *drama triangle* which includes three roles: "the victim," "the villain" and "the hero." People generally recognise this common dynamic immediately. In one corner of the triangle, we have the victim, someone who has been, or feels he or she has been, attacked or victimised. The villain or "persecutor" is the one doing the victimising – real or imagined. And the hero is the one who tries to save the day. Sometimes the victim seeks out a hero, and other times heroes just want to be helpful and jump to fix a situation. No matter where it starts, this dynamic goes round and round in circles. As a hero tries to fix things, he or she often attacks the villain and in that attack, the "villain" becomes a victim and will seek help from another hero. And so it goes.

Systems have an intelligence of their own. If we limit dramas and reactivity, the wisdom of a system will reveal itself. Amazing things happen when people work together in harmony. Even if they don't necessarily like one another, harmony and effective teamwork can take place.

Role Clarity

All systems, tribes or clans have roles. What are the roles that need to be covered in a given organisation, and how are they specified? Often they are filled unconsciously. Systems need to look at the roles required to get their job done. Who needs to be doing what? How do the roles need to be clarified?

All of these elements are presented in an experiential training format where leaders get an intellectual understanding but also have a personal experience of each of the elements. Most of these require some amount of introspection, which is where the real change will begin to take place.

Notes from Chapter 10

- Understand the brain, so you can understand or possibly predict other people's reactions. This helps minimise much reactivity.

- Creating Safety for others is critically important.

- We can learn to recover from limbic reactions – this can be strengthened like a capacity.

- This approach requires each person to develop self-awareness, self-management and self-responsibility.

- Personal development is normal and needed when making changes.

- The Drama Triangle (victim, villain, hero) is a common system dynamic that runs people in circles.

11. Experiential Training and Coaching - the Approach

We propose that any training programme follow an experiential approach. The brain needs the experience in order to really learn. If we're talking about any kind of behaviour change, then this is critical.

We have a special place in our hearts for experiential training, as we have been a part of an avant-garde approach to training for many years. This chapter describes training practices that leverage how the brain learns optimally.

How we learn has been a focus for researchers for decades. We subscribe to basic Adult Learning Theory and have strengthened this approach, as we see those theories being underpinned by neuroscience research.

We need to allow people to learn in such a way that they can implement the new learning or new behaviour when it's needed. They have not only to understand the idea of it, they must also have an experience of it and be able to repeat that experience when needed. Neural pathways are created when we learn a new behaviour. As we practise the new thing, we strengthen the neural pathway. Practice is essential. For training to be effective, it needs to be experiential and focused.

Facilitators and trainers must understand how people learn. They need to keep being aware of what is being learned or not and adjust the pace of learning as needed.

Types of Memory

Memory is key in learning, because if you can't remember something, there's no hope of using it. Let us look at three types of memory: semantic, episodic and procedural.

Semantic memory is where we store facts and information. Traditionally, schools and corporate training programmes have targeted semantic memory. We see information, we hear it, and if we retain it, it will go into our semantic memory so we can recall it at a later date. Books, TED talks and videos are great ways of conveying information, and all of it will be stored in semantic memory until we decide to actually do something with it. We all know people who can recite the best of the best from leadership books, but they do nothing to demonstrate what they know – they don't "walk their talk." A little knowledge for semantic memory can be helpful, but it's far from enough if you want to create change.

Episodic memory is related to semantic memory, but it allows us to remember personal experiences: a time when we learnt something by doing, observing or experiencing it.

Procedural memory allows us to remember *how* to do something, like how to ride a bicycle or a horse. When something is stored in procedural memory, we might not actually understand how it works, remember exactly when we learnt how to do it or be able to speak about how we do it.

In summary, the three types of memory are:

• Semantic: Facts and information

• Episodic: Experiences

• Procedural: What to do

If we want to have any chance of successfully teaching people to do things differently, then any training needs to include procedural memory. It will be helpful for people to have some theory or understanding of what we're training them in, but the key is to get it into procedural memory. The only way to do this is to experience and practise the new behaviour.

If you teach people some concepts, the learning will go into their semantic memory; they might become the world's greatest expert on how to do that thing but be completely unable to put it into practice. A well-executed experiential training will give people positive experiences that they will store in their episodic memory. Because they are positive, successful experiences, people will more likely want to repeat them. If we then want them to be able to recall and use what we teach them, we need to focus on the procedural memory in particular.

Another way to think of experiential learning is this: When we do something once, we create a neural pathway. It's much easier to reinforce an existing neural pathway than it is to create one anew, so it's important to make sure that any training creates the neural pathways (using procedural memory) and then entices and supports people to strengthen them with plenty of practice. In that way, the individuals and teams will be able to build strong neural pathways for the new behaviour.

Yet another way to look at this is with the Edge Model. Before we do something the first time, the new behaviour is over there in the Secondary – on the other side of the edge. If we cross that edge in the training programme, then we know we CAN cross the edge, and it becomes easier a second time. We like to be successful, after all.

We tell people enough about what they're going to learn to satisfy the semantic memory. This will also satisfy their need for certainty and will better create buy-in and reduce resistance. Then we create positive experiences in the training programme, so their episodic memory will have positive associations with new behaviours. But the key to actually learning the new behaviour is the procedural memory. We have people practise in a way that creates a successful use of the new behaviour so that they can use that memory to recall it.

Recall

If we can't recall the new behaviour we're trying to learn, it's useless. Therefore, practice is essential, even if it is done in role-play. The brain doesn't know the difference between a made-up situation and a real one, so you can learn something by practising it in a workshop setting.

As we do this, it will become an unconscious tool that we have in our experiential memory – a habit. The required behaviour will be embedded strongly enough that when it is needed in a situation, our Basal Ganglia will take over and produce it.

If teams learn together, they will be more likely to remember behaviours together as well. We need to leverage the concepts of the social brain and tribe behaviour when we train people together.

Natural Learning

Neuroscientists tell us that the most natural way to learn is to mimic. This is how children learn, and this is why the proverb "Do as I say, not as I do" doesn't work: Children do what their parents do. Employees often will do what their boss and other colleagues do, and participants in a programme will do what the trainers do. It is inherent, unconscious and natural learning. That's part of what makes corporate culture so powerful; it's easy for us to pick up habits from others in the work environment.

In training settings, the trainers must be modelling what they're talking about. Specific demos are helpful, but so is modelling the attitudes and tools of what's being trained every minute of that training. If trainers are teaching people how to be curious and ask questions, it will be counterproductive if they are constantly only telling and never asking questions.

So train by example to enhance the learning process. Every now and again, point out the behaviour, so that people will see it and recognise it consciously.

Pointing Attention

While it's clear that mimicry is a natural learning mode, it is an unconscious process, and we cannot guarantee that people will actually mimic or follow what we want them to. If we want people to consciously learn new a behaviour and choose to use it later, the learning process needs to be a conscious one. Neuroscientists also tell us that it is biologically impossible to learn something that we haven't put our attention on. So in a training programme, especially an experiential programme, point the participants' attention to what it is that you want them to learn.

If there's an experience about team work, and the experience involves a task, people frequently get caught up in the task and pay no attention to the team. It's normal for the brain to do this, but if we point their attention to what's going on in the team, they will be able to see it and learn from it. So point attention before the activity, perhaps during the activity and certainly afterwards. The brain has so many things to pay attention to that we trainers need to get in the habit of pointing attention where it needs to be, so that people can learn the things they came to the course for. If a group is learning together, for example, then pointing attention to what's working will be much more helpful than pointing to what's not working.

116

Set Up for Success

Another element of successful training includes setting people up for success. Teach them something about what they need to know before throwing them into an exercise. Then let them practise enough to be successful with the skill you intend to teach them.

There seems to be a favourite approach amongst trainers to throw people into an exercise in order to let the participants learn how bad they are at something. We believe the intention is to shock them into wanting to do things differently. While this can be a powerful learning experience on occasion, it needs to be used sparingly. This approach does not teach them how to do a new behaviour, even if it creates the appetite for one. It also doesn't create a positive episodic memory or encourage people to look at this behaviour.

Set people up for success so they will want to use their new skill in the future.

Non-Judgement:

Optimal Learning Environment

Judgement creates a limbic reaction that we have to manage. Any time we feel judged, whether by others or ourselves, the brain is busy reacting and/or managing that reaction. As a result, less attention and focus is available for the learning itself. We must be able to try something, fail and allow ourselves to find our way to the "right way" to do something. Any learning environment must therefore be a place where it's safe to try, fail and try again.

Unlearning Habits

We also need to recognise that there might be some very strong neural pathways (habits) that contradict the new behaviour we want to use. If we have a habit of reacting and yelling in response to a given situation, this will continue to be a habitual response until we work on changing it. Let's say we practise responding to those situations more calmly and learn to self-manage in them. We practise and practise, and then a calm response becomes our new habit. There will possibly still be situations where the old habit bursts out of the closet and surprises us. That's because those old neural pathways are still there, and something happened that triggered the old habit. This is part of what makes it hard to use a new behaviour. We have to keep training ourselves to use the newer one and have patience as we learn.

Experiential Training – a Summary

Given how the brain learns and remembers, we recommend experiential learning that is conscious and intentional. Create an environment that is safe, where people can experiment, fail and try again. Make sure they practise the new behaviours that are being taught, and that they have ways to reinforce that behaviour – with their colleagues if possible.

Leverage the social brain; train people in an organisation together, so they can practise forming new habits together. This will reinforce the learning as others become a support system rather than a block to practising new behaviours.

Also, find ways to support individuals in new learning, perhaps with a coach, a buddy, learning groups and training programmes that reinforce their training at a later date. Behavioural change takes time and isn't always easy. People need to be reminded. They need safety: space to fail, where they don't have to get it right for a time.

Recognise that any training, even if it's a technical skills training like using new machinery, requires changes to the brain and a certain amount of personal development. It will also be an edge to cross – maybe a small one or maybe a big one, depending on the nature of the change.

Notes from Chapter 11

- Well-designed, experiential learning programmes create learning that sticks.

- Different types of memory need to be taken into account.

- Procedural memory (using the Basal Ganglia) stores new habits and it's most helpful to create a new habit in the training programme.

- Episodic Memory recalls experiences and it's helpful to have positive, successful experiences in the programme, so there are positive emotional associations.

- Semantic memory records facts. It's not enough to train people about concepts because this type of memory does not help create a new behaviour, even if it helps you understand why you should have a new or different behaviour.

- When this learning is supported by practice and follow-up over time, people can change and culture can change.

- People learn naturally by mimicking.

- Pointing our attention helps us learn intentionally rather than by mimicking.

- Non-judgement is essential for a successful training environment.

- Sometimes we have to unlearn old behaviours in order to learn new behaviours.

12. Individual and Team Coaching

Individual Coaching

It is well known that having follow-up coaching after a training programme improves the retention of the training. Coaching is really a part of the experiential learning process and can be carried out with individuals or with teams.

Personal development takes time. We have to change our thinking, our behaviours and our habits – habits of behaviour. That takes practice and reminders. If we train people in new behaviours, it will be essential to give them the time to adapt, support them, remind them and have patience with them. Coaching can be helpful in all of those.

Coaches need to be aware that coaching is an experiential process as well. How is the coach pointing the attention of the coachee? Are we pointing their attention towards positivity? Are we pointing it towards themselves as powerful individuals, or as an entity in an organisation? Coaches should understand that effective coaching is a powerful, personal growth journey: an experiential journey that the client goes on to learn and have experiences that enhance his or her learning.

We recommend that coaches stay conscious about the pull between the collective and the individual. How does their coaching pull the coachee towards individual desires alone and away from working with the collective?

Team Coaching

Team coaching is also about experiential learning. Team coaching helps a team learn together, notice their habits together and consciously choose to change their culture, their habits and behaviours together. Once there is safety and trust created in a team, there can be a lot of un-doing of behaviours that don't quite work and then implementation of new desired behaviours. Effective team coaches will point the team's attention to what is working and what is not – for the sake of awareness and ability to change.

Team coaching takes place in actual working teams with all the team members, including the team leader, so that the team can become aware of its culture and the relationship dynamics it contains. We are often unaware of how we interact with our teammates and what unconscious habits we have. Only once the team is aware, can it shift. This is the fastest way to increase collaboration. If a team can see how it creates fear together, it can easily reduce that fear and practise different habits that allow more space for collaboration and innovation. And, of course, that will improve results.

Notes from Chapter 12

- Follow up coaching helps retain learning from a training programme.

- Coaching in this programme is about applying the lessons from the programme to each individual's particular work situation.

- Team coaching helps the whole team use the tools from the training programme together.

13. Summary of Our Approach

If we are to be successful in making changes in organisations, we need to keep in mind both the brain and the power of the culture created by the whole system.

Development needs to happen on both the individual and collective levels. We propose an integrated approach: Leadership development and whole culture change. These run concurrently and happen through a combination of training, team coaching and individual coaching. Allow time. Remember that all of the work is ultimately personal development work, and that takes time.

Start by training leaders to understand the basics of the brain and its reactions and need for rewards. Use engaging, brain-optimised learning techniques for training programmes. And once training has begun, use team coaching to embed brain-aware behaviours in the teams. Guide them to create safety and trust. Reduce toxic behaviours and increase positivity. Have teams create agreements together. Have them create clear roles and responsibilities.

Notice where there are silos and/or tribal warfare happening. Bring the teams together. If they haven't yet been trained in brain-friendly working, train them. Provide team coaching for the teams so that together they can move through whatever created their rivalry. Most of the time, rivalries are created because of misunderstandings, fear reactions and ensuing revenge. Both teams need to feel safe, feel good about themselves and understand the others. We need to forgive each other for our reactions. Of course we react. We are human and reactions happen.

Create ways to support individuals in doing the personal work necessary to learn how to manage their brains, whether that is individual coaching, extra trainings, a buddy system or a meditation or relaxation room at the office.

We want to emphasise that training people about the brain must be an experiential training: not just a theoretical understanding, but an in-depth, personal understanding of what goes on in each and every person's brain. Give people the tools to do something different. Every time we need to do something in a new way, it requires us to change our brain. Along with those changes, new mindsets, new ways of thinking, will be required. This *is* personal growth. We need to stop being afraid of it. It is normal, needed, necessary and practical. Our collective fear of "soft skills" is getting in the way of our making the workplace a decent, humane place in which to perform well.

Leadership development in particular is very people-oriented. Leadership is about people and relationships, and it's about being in relationship with others; leadership does not happen in a vacuum. Therefore, our leadership development is very much about personal growth and interpersonal skills. Leaders must be able to control their reactions, to act from a sensible place and not from fear. Leaders also need to understand a bit about how others operate. Some say, and we agree, that a primary job for the leader is to create safety for his or her people so that they can thrive.

Team development using a systemic coaching approach can be extremely helpful in having leadership teams implement their new skills in how to collaborate.

A facilitator can sit in on live meetings and help people relate in ways that are productive and constructive as opposed to reaction generating. Once a team is engaged in a meeting and focused on real topics, their brains will not be focussing on using new behaviours So being there in the moment to support new behaviours along with real meeting topics can have a tremendous impact.

Of course, to be successful in rolling out a more brain-friendly or human-friendly working environment, there needs to be buy-in from the top. If there isn't, some of this can still be achieved. Certainly, a culture can be created within a group, department, division or team as long as the people at the top of those departments are willing, even if their bosses don't treat them the way they would like to be treated.

Collaboration and Innovation

Ultimately, our training results in increased collaboration, innovation and the results that follow. We aim to create environments where people can work together and co-create together with harmony and positivity. The human brain has a natural ability to be creative and to work with others. What gets in the way of collaboration in most organisations is various forms of fear, rooted in the limbic system: Protecting one's turf and recognition, individualism, revenge, tribal warfare and people disliking each other. If our fear circuits are firing too much, we will spend most of our brain's capacity on dealing with our fear, and we won't have anything left over for that creativity and innovation. If we really want to collaborate, we first need to overcome these blocks. It's as simple as that – at least in concept. Enacting that takes practice.

Meanwhile, in Sekhmed

We have looked at what the experiential training and coaching entail. In the next chapters, we will get into more detail about how we approach training, team coaching and individual coaching. To illustrate this, we turn our attention back to Sekhmed.

Kate realises that if Sekhmed is going to improve its results (notably, customer satisfaction), it needs to get more help. Consultants come in to help the team figure out what's going on in their division.

Notes from Chapter 13

- Development needs to happen on individual and team levels.

- Use team coaching on hot spots in the organisation.

- Train leaders to understand the brain.

- Leadership is about relationships between people.

- Knowledge about the brain and about how systems function inform the design, content and delivery of the programmes.

PART 5
The Programme at Sekhmed

14. Preparation

Kate paused for a moment, gathered her poise and opened the door to her large office with a business-like smile. She had been both looking forward to, and apprehensive about, this meeting with the team coaches. She'd tried everything else. This was her last chance to save her position within Sekhmed.

Leanne and Felix settled themselves in the easy chairs Kate had shown them to. Leanne was relaxed, friendly and professional and got straight down to business.

"In preparation for working with the Sekhmed team, we'd like to learn about Sekhmed as a whole from you. You mentioned that you've been very concerned about the lower scores on your customer satisfaction survey. And there's some discontent between the maintenance team and the developers, or Platform and Applications, as you called it," Felix prompted. "What else is going on?"

"A lot of people blame Sales for selling too many options and new applications," Kate said. "That results in instability in the whole division, and the customers are complaining. The cost of the high sales figures is actually a downturn in profits! Then Frank, our head of Maintenance, is aggressive, and people have taken sides against him. And Cedric, the QA manager, has been unable to implement a QA culture and the guys in Maintenance have taken sides over him ..."

Once Kate got started, the words just tumbled out. She felt drained by the time she'd finished – she hadn't realised how badly she needed to let it all out.

Leanne and Felix didn't seem surprised by anything she said. "This kind of thing happens all the time," Leanne reassured her. "You see, it's not Frank by himself who attacks others. The culture supports his attitude and behaviour, and if we're going to get anywhere, the culture needs to be addressed, and everyone needs to work together to change it."

Kate was astonished. That made such sense, but she wouldn't have thought of it herself. They all knew, deep down, that Frank acted as a whip of sorts, galvanising them into action when they could have become a little too complacent. There was clearly a need for someone to take this role – but maybe it wasn't being occupied well.

Felix continued. "The same goes for Iris and the sales team. They're not creating too many sales in a vacuum: there's something in the culture that supports that behaviour as well."

Kate felt a wave of anxiety as his words sank in. Their whole culture was a self-perpetuating mess. And then she slumped. Thank goodness she was no longer doing this on her own. Leanne and Felix inspired her with confidence. Yes, the problem was bigger than she had imagined. But for the first time, she felt she could relax; it was no longer just down to her to sort out the mess she'd walked into a year ago.

Three days later, Leanne and Felix were back in Kate's office to design a plan that would meet Sekhmed's needs.

"We'll start with a one-day session with you and your executive team. It will be a combination of evaluation and coaching. We'll follow that up with a short, two-day leadership development training course, led by Leanne. You can invite any other team leaders and junior executives you're keen to develop, so you'll all be able to use the tools and concepts from that course to understand how to handle the individual issues. I'll back that up with a series of team coaching sessions for the executive team alone, and Toby, one of the coaches in our company, will come in for individual coaching sessions to support the executive team in their development," Felix suggested. "How does that sound to you?"

"Great," Kate answered with mixed feelings. "I'm not sure some of the team will buy into it, though."

"That's okay, we're used to it. We'll take a systems approach and uncover the system dynamics that create the trouble spots," Leanne advised Kate. "We can see there's an edge against implementing QA, and we'll work with the team to help them figure out what's going on there. We know we're going to need to build trust with the executive team before anything else, but we should be able to do that in our initial exec team training session with them." She smiled. "Once they get a glimpse of what's happening beneath the surface, I'm willing to bet they'll all want to know more!"

15. Phase One - Discovery

Kate looked at her executive team at the beginning of their team coaching day. She'd had quite a job to convince them to come and give the process a chance, and there were very mixed levels of interest and buy-in. But, thankfully, everyone agreed that something needed to change, and they all showed up.

Discovery Session

As Leanne and Felix kicked off the facilitated conversation, they observed the team members' attitudes and behaviour.

Frank's sarcasm was clear and pointed, George seemed to be half checked-out and Iris was impatient because she considered she would have been better off working on some new sales calls. Cedric was nervous because he thought he'd caused a lot of the current problems in the team, despite the fact that he was only doing his job, and he was afraid they'd gang up on him. Kate was guarded but generally hopeful that Leanne and Felix would help them make some kind of progress – any kind of progress. Paul was also guardedly hopeful. He wanted to learn more from this day about how he could be a better leader, and he realised he really wanted Sekhmed to succeed.

Felix played their observations back to the team. "Is this how it usually is?"

The expressions around the table ranged from discomfort to surprise to agreement. But the consistent answer around the table was yes, pretty much.

Leanne said, "Ok, so we're going to set some agreements for the rest of our time together. No one will be fired or otherwise punished for what they say during our session." A visible wave of relief spread through the room. "We really want to create as much safety as possible for you all to speak what's true for you. Is there anything else you need in order to do that?"

The atmosphere in the room was definitely more relaxed as Felix and Leanne started a conversation about the organisation.

"Tell us how it got started and what's been happening – both the good stuff and the not-so-good stuff."

"George," Kate smiled encouragingly, "you go first. After all, Sekhmed is your brainchild."

George's expression was a mixture of nostalgia and pride. "It was exciting," he recalled. "We were small, nimble and successful. We had a great reputation for being able to customise, optimise and deliver in a short time. Things were simpler back then – not so much red tape," he pulled a comical face, "and we had a lot of fun."

There was a ripple of laughter around the table. As the others chipped in with their memories, a certain amount of warmth was created around the happy times, and that created a little more space to discuss the areas of difficulty when Leanne moved them on to the not-so-good stuff.

She and Felix made sure that everyone stuck to the ground rules of no blame or other toxic behaviour during that part of the conversation. At first, they had their work cut out, but gradually, everyone was learning how to speak about difficulties without blame. It felt strange, but somehow comforting, for the team to hear about the problems without the usual sarcasm and put-downs.

That conversation was really just a warm up for what needed to happen next. When the Felix and Leanne felt there was enough positivity and safety in the group, they called for a break.

"So …," Leanne looked around the table after everyone had settled back into their chairs. "We're curious about the various attitudes that we noticed at the beginning of the day. We want you to be honest; remember, there will be no repercussions for what you say in these sessions. And remember, too, to stick to our new ground rules: no blame, sarcasm or put-downs. Okay?"

There was a rather cautious nodding of agreement.

Kate cleared her throat. "I'll go first." She chose her words carefully. "I've been feeling overwhelmed by everyone's behaviour. I think there's a lot of childishness in this team. I'm not sure if that's the right name for it, much less how address it. But it's as though we travel to work as adults and turn into children as soon as we walk through the door!"

There was a stunned silence. Then Frank spoke up. "People aren't doing their jobs. Talk about acting like children; I feel I have to crack the whip and keep the pressure up, or nothing will ever get done!" A few mouths opened as though to object, and then they closed again. "I don't always like to be cracking the whip, but it's what I'm paid to do, and it's just how things get done around here. Given everyone else's sloppiness on delivery, it seems necessary. And, well, that's who I am, someone who gets things done!"

"That kind of talk makes me livid," George exploded. "We did just fine before certain people came in and starting messing around with systems that were working perfectly well."

This was a very different George speaking from the one who had had them chuckling over his brainchild just a short time ago. "Everyone used to work well together, meet deadlines and beat sales targets, and we never had a bad atmosphere between us. We built our solid reputation as a market leader on good quality and good service. I created a brilliant software package that is repeatedly being destroyed through the various evolutions the business has gone through and seems to keep going through. A big part of me just wants out of here. Frank's behaviour pisses me off. What rubbish: we never needed a whip before. I hate coming to meetings because Frank just dishes out criticism, and it's destroying the morale of the whole company."

Frank's face was a picture of astonishment – and affront. "It wouldn't be the one thing that got results around here if it weren't necessary," he retaliated. "You're living in the past, George. Maybe it *is* time you left."

"I'd like to remind you all about the ground rules we agreed to a while ago: no blame, sarcasm or put-downs," Leanne said calmly but firmly. "Please don't direct comments like that to each other."

"It's great to get all this stuff out," Felix continued, "but speak to *us* if it's going to be that pointed. Okay? No pointing fingers directly at each other."

Paul broke the awkward silence that followed. "I've been upset by Frank too," he said quietly. "I just want to do a good job, and sometimes all the sniping and name-calling gets me down."

Leanne looked across at Iris. "How about you, Iris?"

"To be honest, I feel like no one appreciates me and all the hard work my team and I do to bring in sales. I have an excellent team, and I can't understand why everyone pushes back on the sales we deliver."

Felix nodded understandingly. "Cedric?"

Cedric fiddled nervously with his pen. "I'm sorry I've been pushing QA on you all. I know you resent it – and me. I thought it was what I was brought in to do." He looked embarrassed as he continued, "I thought I'd been doing better at my job after getting coaching; I don't understand how it seems to have made things worse. I hate thinking that I've rocked the boat."

As one by one they put their issues on the table, Kate noted over and over again how surprised everyone was about each others' opinions. She noticed a glimmer of understanding beginning to emerge – if nothing else, at least an understanding of how bad it had become between them.

It was clear to them all why they weren't collaborating well; they all thought in such different ways and were heading in such different directions! They had some critical opinions of each other too; they didn't respect some individuals, and they didn't respect some roles. They'd made a lot of assumptions. In addition, there was a whole lot of resentment.

One thing Kate knew without a shadow of a doubt: they would never in a million years have said all the things they did, had it not been for the two coaches. At the same time, she could see that they'd all been thinking and feeling these things without expressing them. Throughout all the anger, resentment and pain, Leanne and Felix held the six of them in a safe place where their thoughts and grievances could be expressed honestly for the very first time. Her respect for them was huge.

By the time they broke for lunch, Kate could see that the team realised they were all in this mess together, and that, while it wasn't pretty, they were responsible for creating the mess together in the first place. They were all subdued as they left the room.

The atmosphere was a little less strained after lunch. As soon as Felix realised he had everyone's relatively calm attention, he moved on. "We're going to look at roles this afternoon. Firstly, there are the external roles, or job functions. You can see that they're not all well occupied; for example, there's confusion about Maintenance and about who does what, when."

"And then there are internal, or interpersonal, roles, such as our whip-cracker over here." Leanne nodded at Frank with a questioning smile. "I wonder if Frank might even be a little tired of that role, since he's the one who always has to crack the whip. Cedric used to be peace-keeper, but now the role is mostly unoccupied, so Paul occasionally takes it up. We can see that George thinks vision-setting is his role, and Kate thinks it should be hers. Iris would like to have the role of inspirer, but it's not going too well for her right now." And so it went on, Leanne identifying the internal roles they'd all unconsciously been occupying.

"So …," Paul said slowly, "roles and people are different!"

"Exactly so," Leanne affirmed.

"I get it," Iris chimed in. "So the fact that the guys in Maintenance don't like having QA imposed on them means they don't like the role of QA; yet they've been blaming Cedric personally, which isn't really fair."

"Good noticing, Iris," Felix said as Cedric blushed furiously from the other side of the table.

"I think we've all been finger-pointing in all kinds of directions," Kate commented. "I'd say we've got quite a few things to work on. We really need to clean up our culture. Are you all with me on that?"

Leanne took in all the nods of agreement. "Great. We'll use a systems approach to help you get there. Everything you've been experiencing happens in systems dynamics, and we'll work on the dynamics together later on. We'll also work on role clarification in the team coaching. It's not just Frank –" she looked around the table at each of them. "We look at any of these dynamics as indicators that something in the system wants to change."

Notes from Chapter 15

- Coaches meet with the executive team to find out from the whole team what's happening.

- Coaches begin to create safety by establishing some ground rules.

- The coaches inform the team that they will take a systems approach in their work with them.

- The team learns the basics about roles within a system: roles are distinct from the individuals who inhabit the roles.

- They get messy and bring issues out on the table before attempting to move forward.

16. Phase Two - Leadership Development Programme

The Sekhmed board room had a different atmosphere when the executive team gathered for the training programme. For one thing, it wasn't just them around the table this time; some team leaders and a couple of others who were interested in leadership had been invited to join the training programme. A flip chart stand was positioned to one side of the room, and Leanne stood by it.

"Hi, I'm Leanne Carson, for those of you who haven't met me before." Leanne looked at the faces she didn't recognise, "and in the next couple of days, I'm going to be teaching you all about your brains, and how to manage them."

"*You* won't need to stick around too long then," one of the young team leaders told her neighbour with a grin.

Leanne smiled. "By the time you leave this room, you'll all have a healthy respect for what's going on in your own and each other's brains."

She paused. "For the benefit of those of you who're joining in today, I'd like us to establish the ground rules for how we'll operate together. We set some up at our initial meeting; can anyone remember any of them?"

Kate was mildly surprised when Cedric cleared his throat. "No sarcasm, blaming, judgement or put-downs. This has to be a safe space for us all to learn in."

"Thank you." Leanne nodded. "Do we have agreement on those?" She looked around the room. "Anything to add?"

"What does 'no judgement' mean, exactly?" Kirsty, one of the young team leaders, asked. "Will any of this show up in our year end reviews?"

"No, absolutely not," Kate jumped in. "We're all in this together. We're all learning together – for ourselves and for the sake of Sekhmed – and nothing we say in this room gets judged or evaluated. That's the whole point, that we can use this as a kind of … of practice ground, where we get to make mistakes, do things wrong, figure things out in our heads … so that when we're outside the training room, we can do things better."

"So …," Kirsty asked thoughtfully, "how about adding something around there being no repercussions after this is over?"

"You *will* see each other – and yourselves – differently after you've been through the training," Leanne pointed out. "But there won't be any repercussions from management. Is that ok?"

Kirsty nodded silently.

Leanne wrote the words *No Sarcasm, No Blaming, No Judgement, No Put Downs, No Evaluation,* on the flip chart. "Let's kick off with a look at Leadership."

Leadership

Leanne explained that leadership is more about people than managing tasks. "Leaders need to empower teams, both as a system and as individual team members, and they need to understand something about human beings if they're going to lead them."

It wasn't only the younger team leaders who were learning about leadership.

Oh, I get it, Kate realised uncomfortably at the end of the Leadership session. *I've been focussing on tasks more than relationships. I thought I was good at relating to people, but I can see now that that's not the same thing. And judging by the looks on some of the other faces, I'm not the only one!*

Neuroscience and Self-Management:

"Now, we're going to learn some basics about how the brain works," Leanne said, drawing a simple picture of the human brain on the flip chart. "The first thing I want you to know is that emotional reactions are normal, and they happen all the time. They're chemical; it's what our brains do. Plain and simple."

Kate noticed a variety of reactions around the room, ranging from amazement to puzzlement.

"I thought brains did the thinking, not the feeling stuff," Paul confessed.

"We all have these limbic triggers of belonging, status, fairness, autonomy and certainty – all of us," Leanne said as she wrote the words up on the flip chart in bright red capital letters.

She proceeded to describe the human limbic system and how reactions happened. "Depending on our background, past experiences and personalities, some of us will react more strongly to some of the triggers than we will to others. The important thing is for us to learn how to manage ourselves so that we're not run by our emotional reactions."

Leanne turned over a sheet on the flip chart to uncover a list she'd made earlier. "There are three great tools we can learn to use." She gave them a minute to read through the points:

Labelling: Taking time to notice how I think and feel about something before acting.

Reappraising: I can choose my mindset. If we change our minds, we re-train our brains.

Mindfulness/non-judgmental awareness: Looking at things without assumptions or judgement.

The training programme was experiential, practical and very engaging, and for the rest of the morning, they practised recovery techniques for the limbic reactions with one another.

First, they created situations where they imagined being triggered by one another. Leanne made it easy to explore how their brains drove them in various ways.

Oh, so that's what was happening in Iris's brain when I asked questions that I thought would help build up our relationship, Kate realised, squirming silently.

She could tell from the expressions around her that there was a good deal of discomfort as they each discovered how they were triggering each other and how their limbic system was reacting and creating emotional responses within them that then led to more triggering behaviour. But with the safety of their ground rules, they were able to be really curious about themselves and how they were operating at work.

Leanne showed them how to label and reappraise, so they could calm their own reactions. They learned one important lesson while practising reappraisal in particular: pretty much everyone had a positive intention. When they learned to use this to reappraise their reactions, they relaxed quite quickly. It got them out of blame and the other reactions that normally followed.

"OK, so now I'd like to teach you about a really powerful recovery technique. Has anyone heard of mindfulness practice?" Leanne asked.

"Isn't that a kind of meditation?" Iris asked, adopting a saintly, spaced-out pose and humming Om. There was a ripple of laughter around the room.

"Yes and no," Leanne replied with a smile. "We're not trying to reach Nirvana here. It's such a great recovery technique that anyone can use, anytime, anywhere. Instant access, even without Wifi."

There was more laughter, and then Frank leaned back in his chair and waved a hand dismissively. "Oh, for God's sake. Just tell me how long you're going to play games for, and I'll come back when you've finished. I have better things to do with my –"

"Come on, Frank!" Iris's voice rang out. Everyone looked at her, including Frank. "We all agreed we'd be in this together. It's the only way out of the mess we're in. Give it a chance."

"It might seem airy-fairy," Leanne looked at everyone, not just Frank. "But we're actually training the brain. It's science we're dealing with here, neuroscience." Her voice was pleasant and business-like. "Shall we start? Just get yourselves comfortable," she invited them all.

As they all shuffled around in their chairs, their attention moved away from Frank, and he sank back into his chair. Kate took a deep, if shaky, breath.

Skilfully, Leanne led them through an exercise of non-judgemental awareness, or mindfulness practice, as she called it.

"Close your eyes and take a moment to just relax." After a minute, Leanne continued in a quiet, calm voice. "Notice that thoughts show up in your mind ... Just notice them and notice you can choose to follow them or not ... Notice that it's so easy to judge a situation or a thought – oh that's good or bad ... In this practice, just try noticing without any good or bad, without any right or wrong ... Simply let your thoughts pass by ... The practice of mindfulness is being able to notice without judgment.

"Let's make it a little more challenging," Leanne carried on. "Recall a situation where you would normally react ... Now imagine yourself being in that situation and just noticing what's happening – without judgement ... There's no good or bad," she commented, "no right or wrong ... Things are happening and you can watch them without judgement ... Notice that you also have thoughts about what's happening – you can even observe your thoughts without judgement ... Give yourself another minute to just observe your thoughts without doing anything with them – just notice."

Then she brought their attention back to the room and gave them a moment to take it all in. The atmosphere was surprisingly spacious and relaxed.

"What was that like?" Leanne asked when they'd all had a good stretch.

"That's cool!" Iris exclaimed. "It was really easy."

"Much easier than getting stressed out," Paul agreed enthusiastically.

"That's all very well, but how can we be non-judgemental when there are things going wrong all around us?" Frank asked, a little begrudgingly. "Surely we have to judge if something works or not?"

Like the Maintenance and QA problems, Kate thought to herself, *not to mention the Sales challenges.*

"That's a great question, Frank," Leanne responded. "As you'll see when you've had a chance to practise it a bit, discernment is different from judgment. You can *discern* whether something is working or not. But if you label it good or bad, right or wrong, that turns it into judgement and actually makes the thing more difficult to work with. If there's an atmosphere of positivity and collaboration, people can admit that something isn't working, and if they continue to be non-judgemental about it, it will be much easier to change."

"We'd be working like a team!" Cedric ventured.

There was a stunned silence as they all realised what that meant.

"But will it work when we're in the middle of a real situation?" Paul asked.

"You'll get some support individually so that you can learn how to make it work in the real situations you each come across," Leanne reassured him. "We'll start that phase of this programme in a couple of weeks. You've seen that it can work. Remember what I told you about the brain? It doesn't know the difference between a made-up situation and a real one, so you can learn something by practising it in another setting. When you do it enough times, it will become an unconscious tool that you have in your experiential memory – a habit. The new behaviour will be embedded strongly enough that when it is needed in a real situation, your Basal Ganglia will take over and produce it."

"Cool," Iris said again in a tone of respect. "The brain is amazing."

Leanne smiled. They were getting it.

There was a decidedly reflective air in the room as the day's training came to an end.

Change

"Let's take a look at Change," Leanne said the following morning.

"Change is difficult for any brain to manage, and it's uncomfortable, by default." She moved to the flip chart. "The Edge Model helps us to understand what's going on when changes are taking place."

Leanne wrote Primary on the flip chart. "This is where we are now, how we identify ourselves or how we do things at the moment." Then she wrote Secondary. "Any ideas?" she asked, looking around.

"What happens next? Where we want to go?" Cedric offered uncertainly.

"Spot on," Leanne affirmed. "Secondary contains all the unknown possibilities of how we could be, or could do things – perhaps a desired state or a sense of what we need to become in the future. So to get from Primary to Secondary, we have to cross an edge."

Leanne wrote Edge on the flip chart. "An edge could be as small as returning to our desk from a meeting, or as large as facing retirement."

"How about coming on a leadership training programme?" Paul asked. "Is that an edge?"

"You bet," Leanne nodded. "Then there are individual edges and collective edges, such as a startup seeing that it's getting bigger and needing more processes and procedures." She paused a moment to let the example sink in, "To make matters even more exciting, when any team or system is at an edge, everyone inside it is also brought to an individual edge."

A whole lot of murmuring broke out. "Oh – my – God," Iris exclaimed with a mock-dramatic expression. "I'm at an edge!"

Kate grinned – she was learning to enjoy the way Iris brought her personality to the room.

"My edge is definitely different from your edge," George said slowly, "and yet we're all in a collective edge together as well."

There was silence in the room as they all digested what they were learning.

Leanne brought the focus back to the flip chart. "As you can see, the difficulties are compounded when we start talking about change involving many individuals. So in addition to paying attention to our own brain reactions, it will be useful to pay attention to the collective – Sekhmed – and its current culture.

"There are so many possibilities for Secondaries, all of them on the other side of the edge, and we can't quite see them from where we are in the Primary," Leanne explained. "Crossing an edge – making a change – can be quite difficult. We're moving from the known to the unknown, and as we know from neuroscience, the brain doesn't like that; it's not a comfortable place to be."

"You're not kidding," George stated emphatically.

Leanne nodded. "A lot of things can happen at an edge, for example: excitement, resistance, drama and toxic behaviours. We call them Edge Behaviours, and they're useful to know about because when we see them simply as *behaviours*, we can realise that a person or a system is at an edge and get curious about the edge itself, rather than react against the person having the behaviour."

"I didn't understand why I was feeling so annoyed. Now I can see that all the changes we've had recently have been messing with my mind," one of the team leaders said. A couple of the others murmured their agreement. "It's been really disorienting."

"I can see we've been pushing changes on people without realising the impact," Cedric acknowledged.

What else are we going to discover? Kate wondered, a little subdued. *I had no idea all this stuff was going on in the company or that leadership depended so much on who we are and the quality of our interactions, rather than what we do and how well we do it.*

146

Social Intelligence

"The brain's focus on survival drives us to be protective of our needs and fearful of perceived threats," Leanne said. "Additionally, the brain is a social brain, designed to be in relationship with others. You can probably see that you're likely to get problems when people come together in groups, especially if they believe – or the limbic system perceives – they're not safe and secure. Groups in organisations are no different. Many of the challenges in organisations stem from our survival-based needs and fears, based on the limbic system's desire for survival and rewards that we discussed earlier. Some of those needs include belonging, status, fairness, certainty and autonomy." She listed them under NEEDS on the flip chart and looked around the room. "What are some things people might have fears or worries about in groups?"

"Fear of failing?" Kate volunteered.

"Fear of not being good enough?" Cedric asked cautiously.

"Fear of the unknown," Paul stated.

"How about fear of not being appreciated by others?" Iris asked.

Leanne was nodding and writing the suggestions up on the flip chart under a separate list headed FEARS. "And that's just for starters," she said. "You'll notice that those needs and fears are all individual concerns, and they are all survival-based at some level, but they can only exist in relation to other individuals."

She turned back to the group. "So how easy is it to be creative when you're all tied up in knots?" she asked.

"It's not," George said. "If you're always wondering who's going to shoot your ideas down or criticise you, you're hardly likely to feel safe enough to risk putting your ideas out there."

"Thanks, George." Leanne wrote the word SAFETY up on the flip chart. "People need to feel safe in order to feel creative; they'll be less likely to share ideas and appreciate other ideas – things that are necessary for collaboration – unless they feel safe.

"However," she went on, "as you now know, reacting is normal, even if it's not useful, and reactions are contagious. You're all just triggering each other's limbic systems. So from now on, you can notice how others are acting or reacting, and try to get in touch with how your own behaviour might actually have created a reaction. And you need to use your own self awareness and self management to evaluate your level of reaction."

Systems Dynamics

"That leads us nicely into how members of groups interact with each other," Leanne informed them. "We call that Systems Dynamics. Every group of people has a *culture*, a set of habits of how things are done, and each one of those habits can be difficult to change."

She told them how tribes operate and how cultures are created quite quickly between the habit-making part of the brain and the ways we tend to operate in tribes. "Groups or systems also have a wisdom of their own. And unfortunately, they can also have some toxic behaviour patterns."

She turned to the flip chart and wrote up Blame, Criticism, Contempt and Stonewalling in large red letters, then she proceeded to define them. "Everyone uses these from time to time. You need to be aware of them because they can cause real problems – in your work life and your personal life. They're really important, and you'll go into them in more detail in your team coaching sessions, but for now, can you all see which one or ones you default to?"

There was a subdued nodding from around the table. "Take a moment to write down a few notes of self reflection," she suggested. "And remember, these are survival-based habits that we've all learned at some point in our lives, so it's not helpful to beat ourselves – or anyone else, for that matter – up about having them!"

Leanne wrote Drama Triangle on the flip chart and drew a triangle beneath it. "Let's play a game," she said in a purposefully upbeat tone. "In one corner of the triangle, we have the Victim," she explained, "someone who has been, or feels he or she has been, attacked or victimised."

She wrote Villain at one of the other corners. "The Villain, or Persecutor, is the one doing the victimising – real or imagined."

She wrote Hero at the last corner. "The Hero saves the day. But no matter where it starts, this dynamic goes round and round in circles. As the hero tries to fix things, he or she often attacks the villain – not physically, of course – and then the villain becomes the victim and will look for help from another hero."

They had a great time playing this out in various games. At the same time, they recognised its prevalence in Sekhmed. In the games, they learned to step out of the triangle and take full responsibility for themselves, their own situations and reactions.

When Leanne taught them about rank and revenge, they could see that a lot of what was happening in response to Cedric and the QA system was really about revenge.

"Would you be okay if we look at the situation around QA to show how this works?" Leanne asked Cedric.

Cedric nodded a bit uncertainly.

"Thanks, Cedric." She turned her attention from him to the others. "As I understand it, Kate brought Cedric into Sekhmed because she felt the company had grown large enough to need some proper QA systems."

Kate nodded.

"From everyone else's perspective, this young, friendly guy arrived out of nowhere and automatically had a certain rank, purely because he had a fancy title and a position with The Corporation. At first, Cedric backed down very easily during conflict because he was a nice guy, but after some assertiveness training, he was learning to stand in his authority, and he had started telling people what to do. To many people, it felt like he was out of place, over-stepping his bounds and unconsciously barging into their territory. Their revenge showed up in a number of ways including stonewalling, or ignoring him, for example, and in some cases, even actively undermining what he was attempting to do."

It wasn't only Cedric who was feeling uncomfortable at this point.

"All these dynamics – drama triangles, revenge and toxic behaviours – are possibly all edge behaviours which are just indicators that the system is at an edge," Leanne reminded them. "The team coaching will explore edges more and help you to cross them or let them go."

For the last hour of the training day, they discovered how useful and important positivity is. "There's much more to it than the feel-good factor. It actually makes a big difference to your productivity, creativity and how you interact and collaborate." Leanne showed them a number of ways to get there, including recovering from their limbic reactions.

"It's not about removing conflict but about learning how to have *productive* conflict," she said as she drew the training session to a close. Everyone in the room now understood that they needed to create a culture together that they would all appreciate and want to be a part of, and that this would naturally bring positivity and create a foundation from which they could have more collaboration.

They also knew that knowing that was only a small first step and that they really had some work to do to implement it. They were relieved to learn that they would be supported in that implementation by individual and team coaches.

Notes from Chapter 16

- Leanne leads a two-day leadership programme based on neuroscience.

- Leadership happens in relationship.

- Leaders need to learn about the brain for their own self-management but also because they need to be conscious about their impact on others.

- Limbic reactions happen because we're human.

- Labelling, reappraising and mindfulness are ways the PFC can manage the limbic system.

- The Edge Model is a model for change. There are collective and individual edges.

- Edge behaviours are just indicators that something is changing or that there is resistance to change.

- The brain is a social brain – highly tuned to be in relationship with others. There is a lot of fear involved in those relationships with others.

- System Dynamics include toxic behaviours, drama triangles, rank and revenge.

- This work isn't about removing conflict but having productive conflict.

17. Phase Three - Personal Work and Systems Coaching

Kate had asked the executive team to stay on after Leanne and the others left the training room. She could sense a much more positive atmosphere between them already.

"Felix will be taking our team coaching sessions," she told them after they'd chatted informally about the training they'd had with Leanne. "And Toby, another of their coaches, will be seeing us individually to help us work through whatever would be most helpful to us. *I want to reiterate that I won't have any feedback from Toby about what you discuss in your one-to-one sessions with him*," Kate stressed. "The format for each of us will be the same, though. We'll each create a plan with Toby about how to shift mindsets and behaviours and how to practise mindfulness and non-judgemental awareness. Then we'll set objectives about how to implement the learning from the leadership training. It's all going to take place in the context of Sekhmed's need for us to work as a team, which I think we now agree is essential."

Personal Work

Kate knew the coaching wouldn't be individualistic, like the life coaching she'd had years ago when her coach had asked her about her personal dreams and goals and then helped her to work out how to get there. Instead, Toby would be working with them to find out how they wanted to implement what they'd learned in the leadership programme, and what dreams they had within Sekhmed. It would use the language of the leadership training and help them implement those aspects of personal development.

But Kate was aware that it might still be possible for members of the team to discover their own dreams, and that they couldn't work at Sekhmed any longer.

Systems Coaching

Felix worked with the whole executive team as their team coach to help them get clearer about how they were using their brains together. Although this was a continuation of the work they had started in their initial session with Felix and Leanne, now, with the benefit of all they had learned in the training programme with Leanne, it felt very different.

Team Coaching Session One – Noticing Impact

"We'll be continuing the work we started in the initial session when I came with Leanne, and the work you did with her in the training course," Felix told the executive team. "Let's just run through the agreements we created together during our initial session." He looked around the room. "Would someone like to remind us all?"

Paul jumped straight in. "No sarcasm, blaming, judgement or put-downs, and no evaluation from management."

"Thanks. Does anyone want to add anything?" Felix checked as he wrote the agreements up on the flip chart.

"These sessions are confidential," Cedric said, "and no one will be evaluated by what happens in them."

"Thank you." Felix added them to his list. "We're going to be taking a systems approach," he continued. "You learned the basics in the leadership training course, and you'll each work on your personal self awareness, self management and self responsibility in your sessions with Toby. That, of course, includes noticing your own reactions, using recovery techniques and taking responsibility for your own actions. These team coaching sessions are to help you apply what you learned on the training course at the team level. So using the systems thinking, we'll look, with as much non-judgement as possible, at how reactions happen, knowing that our brains are just responding to each other in systemic fashion."

The team started to get real with one another about their systems dynamics. They looked at the roles they were holding – or not; at what roles were needed and how they could be held in a way that was sustainable. Frank and the group decided that it probably wasn't good for all of them that he was the whip-cracker, and they decided to share that role.

"Maybe some of us can learn some lessons from Frank about that," Cedric suggested tentatively.

"Good idea. We're going to focus on roles in one of the later team coaching sessions, so can we put that aside until then?" Felix asked. "Let's look at some of the needs within the team first. We can start with Status."

Most of the team members recognised their own need for Status, and how they were worried about losing their jobs, position or prestige. Frank was surprised that he, too, recognised his need for status.

"How about Belonging?" Felix asked.

George, Paul, Iris and Cedric talked about how much they really wanted to belong. The rest of the team were really surprised that George wanted to belong.

"I thought you wanted to be shot of Sekhmed," Iris declared. "You always seem so fed up with us all. And when you clam up, it's like you're judging us, or blaming us, or something."

155

George was shocked to hear that his silence triggered reactions in other people. "I thought I was staying out of the way and that being quiet was going to help," he responded defensively.

"Remember," Felix explained, "our brains make up reasons for everything we experience. So given the fear circuitry in all brains, the team reacted to your quietness and just assumed the worst."

"So ... when I talked about feeling pissed off with Frank during our initial meeting with you and Leanne," George considered thoughtfully, "... when Frank said he had to crack the whip in order for things to get done ... I was feeling that my status and belonging – and my sense of control too, I guess – were all being threatened by Frank ... and probably also by the demise of Sekhmed in general."

Felix nodded.

"And I wasn't just doing it to myself in a vacuum. It was all the social brain reacting to what other people were doing." George shook his head incredulously. "How easy it is to react! All I wanted at the time was revenge."

"Any others?" Felix looked around the room.

"I've felt really intimidated by Frank," Paul confessed. "I come to work to do a good job and hopefully to feel good about it too, not to wonder when I'm going to be humiliated or criticised again."

"Intimidated? That's absurd." Frank was dismissive. "I know most people are jealous of my logic and power, but all this talk of fear, intimidation and revenge is rubbish. I was just serving the company the best way I could!"

"It's surprising, isn't it, how people experience us in ways we couldn't have imagined," Felix commented mildly.

There was a long silence as what he said sunk in.

"Does anyone remember the work you did on drama triangles?" Felix asked. "What are some of the more common examples you are aware of within Sekhmed?"

Kate sighed. "I guess my efforts to solve the problems all on my own was me stepping into a hero role."

"Say more about that," Felix invited.

"Well …," Kate said thoughtfully. "I really wanted to be a good boss and save Sekhmed … but for me to be the hero, there had to be a victim and a persecutor … and it really just perpetuated some drama triangles instead of solving anything." She paused. "I guess I was trying to fix everything on my own. Was that about increasing my sense of status?" It was a big realisation, and Kate was aware that she was making herself very vulnerable by disclosing it, but she knew that her willingness to be vulnerable would make it easier for the rest of her team to do the same. She could also see how much more leverage she would have if they all worked together as a team. What a relief that would be! She sighed.

"Thank you for your honesty and openness," Felix nodded slowly, his gaze taking in everyone's reactions as he held the space and made sure no one would attack Kate in her most vulnerable moment.

"Oh my God!" Iris's voice crashed into the silence. She looked as though she'd just had a revelation. "I'm a hero-junkie!"

Everyone looked at her in surprise.

"I guess I always want to save the day too," she confessed. "I must have a thing about Status as well. Can you have two heroes? Maybe Kate and I are competing for hero status!"

"Let's explore some of the drama triangles and look at other ways you could handle those situations," Felix suggested.

As they discussed the various relationships, there was surprise, resistance, some anger and even a bit of laughter.

"So Cedric was becoming the victim, Frank was the villain and Kate was trying to fix it," Paul reflected. "Or…" he frowned thoughtfully. "Maybe I was trying to fix it." And so it continued.

"Before we end this session," Felix said, "I'd like you all to make some agreements about how you're going to be more aware of reactions and begin to manage them so you can be intentional about how this team operates."

They agreed to do the personal work necessary to notice their own reactions and to manage them. "We could also support each other in noticing if and when reactions do go flying around the table," Kate suggested.

"Maybe in those times, we can take a pause and just step back for a few minutes, or maybe we can take a short break," Iris added.

"You also need to agree to not judge or blame others for reactions," Felix said, "but instead give a little room for reactions, and in some cases make requests for different behaviour styles. "At least," he urged, "have a conversation about how reactions go. It's about sharing responsibility for your team behaviours."

"Let's spend a few minutes appreciating each other," Felix said finally.

Talk about an edge!

"I want to appreciate everyone's willingness to spend time together looking at all this stuff, even though some of it – well, quite a lot, actually – has been uncomfortable," Kate announced.

Iris looked across at Kate. "You've always been the first one to do the hard thing during these sessions."

Kate swallowed hard. "Thanks, Iris. You always take such good care of your team, and you work really hard to bring money into Sekhmed."

The team knew by now that this was specifically about increasing their positivity. It was a little uncomfortable for them, but it still created a lot of dopamine from limbic rewards. The first team coaching day had definitely been a feel-good session.

Between Team Coaching Sessions

All the team members worked individually with Toby to continue the personal development necessary to manage their reactions, to learn to appreciate, to be better team members and anything else that came up for them.

Paul saw how his need for belonging (to George in particular) kept him from doing his job honestly from time to time. He also realised that fairness was a big driver for him. He hated it when Frank picked on others, especially on George; it always seemed so unfair. Combined with his need for belonging, it created such powerful reactions and feelings of resentment and revenge, it was almost shocking.

But how interesting it was to realise that fairness was a deep-seated emotional response in the brain. And also that it was partly mirror neurons at work, because it wasn't even that Frank was attacking him personally. Most of the time, Frank attacked George and Iris, but Paul could see that he was still reacting as though Frank was attacking him!

Toby helped him find ways to reappraise the situation and practise recovering from this particular reaction. Paul noticed that it helped him change his attitude and significantly lessened his anger at Frank. He also knew he was going to have to move towards independence in a way. He would have to say "No" to George at times. That was going to be hard, but he saw that it was necessary.

Cedric also got some new awareness about belonging from his work with Toby, and various pieces were starting to fall into place. It was clear that his need for belonging had prevented him from stepping into a place of authority, and he started to find new ways to work with people on QA.

They all agreed to meet for a short period each week specifically to review and strengthen their sense of team.

They succeeded and they failed. They had a few fights, but fortunately no one gave up. They recognised their reactions more and began to self manage a little better in their meetings. Rather than investing any time in blaming colleagues, some of them learned to blow off steam in other ways. They had the seeds of seeing each other's roles. They were learning that appreciation worked wonders and also felt great. It was still a bit uncomfortable, but they could see the payoff.

Team Coaching Session Two – Who Are We?

"How's it been going since our first session?" Felix asked the executive team.

"Well," Kate said into the silence, after giving the others a chance to speak first. "We've been working on calming our reactions to each other."

"They haven't exactly stopped happening," Paul said.

"But we do seem to be handling them better," Iris put in.

"The atmosphere seems more positive," Cedric added.

"I guess we're work in progress," George commented drily.

"That's a great way to put it," Felix replied. "I can already hear a difference in the way you're talking to each other. Do I have your permission to point out any toxic behaviour and reactions as we work together today?"

He took in their nods. "Thank you. You learned about the Edge Model during the training course with Leanne. Let's take another look at it and see what is Primary for your system here at Sekhmed. How do you define yourselves as an organisation?"

"Flexibility," George said. "We're nimble, able to respond to our customers' demands –"

"And that's the problem!" Frank interrupted. "It gets us into trouble all the time, bending backwards to promise customers things we can't deliver."

"Well, yes," Kate agreed thoughtfully. "I suppose it's a fantasy to think Sekhmed is still like that. It's a larger company now, with sixty employees instead of the six it started out with, and we need to start behaving like one."

As arguments about what was good and what wasn't flared up, Felix pointed out the reactions that were happening. "This is a systemic edge," he told them. And with his help, they were able to have a discussion about it. They noticed that they had successfully had an open disagreement without making it personal and without attacking each other.

"Notice your own reactions," Felix invited. "Where's the edge?"

"It's hard to accept that we really aren't a startup anymore," George said slowly, his shoulders hunched in defeat. "I suppose it's a huge edge."

"It can actually feel like physical pain to recognise that you aren't what or who you thought you were," Felix told them. "It's like grief. We need to acknowledge the shift and grieve the loss of the old ways."

"It's not my baby any more," George sighed.

"More like a rebellious teenager!" Paul said with a wry smile. "Do you remember how you came up with the name Sekhmed?"

"I named her after Sekhmet, the Egyptian goddess of healing," George informed them proudly, "since we were creating software for the medical industry."

As Paul and George relived old memories, with Frank throwing in the odd comment here and there, everyone else got a feel for Sekhmed as it was at the beginning.

Iris, who had been tapping away at her phone, looked up with a grin. "I've just discovered that Sekhmet was more a goddess of power than of healing. And apparently, she had quite a temper!"

Even Frank laughed then. "I think we should focus on her softer side," he said, which prompted even more laughter.

"Gosh, George, it must be really difficult for you, having us all charge in with our ideas of how to change your company," Cedric observed. "I can understand now why people have been resisting QA." He knew that at first, he had been very shy about his job, and then he had tried forcing people to follow the QA procedures and processes. "It's like … I was trying to stuff you all into a cage when you thought of yourselves as free birds."

"I wish I'd known some of this before," Iris declared. "I feel I understand Sekhmed so much better – and you too, George. I had thought that if I – my sales team and I – just made enough sales, we'd be able to help Sekhmed get over this … this blip in its successful history. But I can see that even if I wasn't around in the very beginning of Sekhmed's existence, I had kind of bought into that identity of it as a startup that could create any apps it wanted to. I was training my sales people to operate that way too: fast, and doing anything the customer wanted."

She gave a big sigh. "I'm just realising that today's Sekhmed isn't quite so nimble, that selling all those variants isn't really helpful to the

162

whole … system. It might pad my team's bonuses, but it hurts the overall bottom line," she said regretfully. "But seeing Sekhmed in this new light helps me to see its … its solidity. It's like," she mused, "there's a certain power in the feeling of being established, which gives us the ability to actually say 'No' to a customer's whim."

Kate listened with a growing admiration for her executive team. She'd learned so much about them through the few days of this training process that she hadn't got anywhere near to finding out in the whole year she'd been with the company. *And it's not just the people here*, she realised. *Everyone has some of this stuff going on. Everyone I know has reactions based on the reactions of others.*

She thought about how conflicts began. *No wonder we were stuck – we don't know who we are. I've got my work cut out for me,* she thought. *But as long as we work together, we'll make it.*

"Ok," Felix said after the break, "I'd like you to rate yourselves for individualism on a scale of 1-10."

After a minute, he continued, "Now rate each other. You can write on these," he said as he passed round some pieces of paper, "and before you show each other your ratings, remember that this is a judgement-free zone."

The results were fascinating. Cedric had rated everyone except for Kate as very individualistic. Most of them had ranked Cedric and Kate as team focused and George and Iris as extremely individualistic.

"I'm surprised that people think I'm individualistic," George admitted.

"Would you like to hear what made people come up with that rating?" Felix asked.

As he thought through the assessment, George admitted that it was consistent with what he had worked on with Toby in his individual coaching session. "I know that status, autonomy, control and independence are all very important to me. I'm beginning to see that all of that means I'm not really a great team player." It all made sense, even if it was a surprise.

Paul was given a wide mix of ratings.

"And most of you have rated Frank more towards team focus than individual," Felix concluded.

"That is weird!" Iris blurted out and then caught herself. "I don't mean that rudely, really. It's just … ." She was clearly struggling to understand.

"Frank can be tough, trying to get results no matter what," George agreed, "and he can be a little caustic, but he always had the good of the organisation in mind … at least, he did in the past. Until things started to fall apart, I was amazed how he'd often spend all his breaks talking about technical stuff with his team and how they could make things even better."

Frank looked as though he didn't know what to do with himself. Everyone was looking at him with a new sense of appreciation. He got a status boost just by discovering how much influence he really had.

I could have had a lot more impact and could influence a lot more if I left sarcasm and criticism behind and was a little more understanding, he realised, taken aback by everyone's appreciation of him. *Maybe this is how I can use my coaching sessions with Toby better.* He'd stubbornly just stuck to data and complaints in his first session because it was safe ground. *But perhaps I could get these status boosts without having contempt for others by being the one who keeps people focussed on the team's goals.*

164

It was all beginning to make sense. He had begun to admit to himself that he was addicted to power and control, ever since that session on how the brain worked. Perhaps that coach really could help him change his power/control default mechanism. *It will be hard to let go of that habit; I've lived with it for so long – ever since my army days. Maybe even before that ... perhaps that was what attracted me to the army in the first place!*

Facing the enemy within actually takes every bit as much courage as facing the enemy on the ground, he thought soberly, vowing to be a little more forthcoming in the next session with Toby. *And maybe I'd get along better with my family as well. God knows I need to.*

With Felix facilitating, they spent some time discussing the results of the assessments and looked at how they could become more of a team. They all agreed that they would give it a try.

Felix asked them to work together on creating a collective identity. "How do you want to operate? What is the culture you want to create? Are you still a flexible startup?"

The team had an honest discussion about how they needed to unify around their identity.

"Some individualism might need to be put on the back burner," Kate mooted.

"What about job security?" Paul asked.

"I got buy-in from The Corporation that no one would be fired," Kate reassured them.

"What about our sales bonuses?" Iris asked. "Does that create too much individualism?"

"We need to put that aside for the moment, Iris," Kate replied, "but I promise we'll discuss it over the next month. "We also need to discuss how sales are made," she added.

"I've been thinking about that," Iris admitted. "My sales people can be pretty gung-ho about getting new business, and they love the friendly sales competitions. But I can see that the way we've been selling might not be serving the whole system. I was thinking … " she sounded a little cautious, "maybe I could work with George and Paul to set some realistic guidelines for what the company can promise, not just what the sales team or the individual applications engineers can promise." She looked uncertainly at them.

"That's a good idea," George agreed.

Paul nodded. "Maybe the three of us could meet in the next two or three weeks and talk it through."

"Sure," Iris said. "And I'll need to sit down with my sales team and share with them what we've been discussing." She looked straight at Felix. "I'm guessing that any changes I put to the sales team will put them at an edge."

"You've got it," Felix said. "You'll need to be conscious about how you open that discussion with them."

"If I slap limits on them, I'm certain they'll have a massive reaction, and that will create a tribal revenge, won't it?"

Kate was impressed by the way her team were applying so much of what they'd just learned.

"Let's take another look at Sekhmed's current strengths and where you want to grow as a company," Felix suggested.

"We do want more market-share," Paul said.

"And we definitely want to increase customer satisfaction," Frank added.

Between Team Coaching Sessions

Over the following month, the executive team met and decided on some characteristics that they wanted for Sekhmed.

"Flexibility within reason," Iris suggested, "like an athlete … or an amateur gymnast, but not a contortionist."

"High-quality," George said firmly.

"How could I not agree," Cedric said with a sheepish grin.

"So we all agree that we want to be known for high-quality software," Kate declared when they'd all spoken. "It's obviously a stretch for us at the moment, but I think your suggestions for getting buy-in from the rest of the organisation will get us there."

"We'll need to allow enough time to work on this," Cedric said cautiously.

"We can't just slap it on our teams," Paul agreed, "but we must create a shared vision for why we're heading in this direction."

"It could be inspiring," Kate said. "Great customer relationships from sales to service."

"That doesn't mean the customers can have every little thing they want," Frank interjected, "but if we have good relationships, the customers will understand that consistency and bug-free code is more important than having every little desire met."

Amazing, Kate thought, over and over again. *Bloody amazing.*

The team also met with Toby again to continue practising recovery techniques. Frank was shocked to find himself using mindfulness meditation for a few minutes now and again – something he thought was for sissies and weirdos. He would have died rather than tell anyone that was what he was doing, of course, but he found quite quickly that it was helpful for his sanity and helpful in holding back his whip and criticisms of the others.

Team Coaching Session Three – Roles, Rank and Revenge

"It's good to see you all," Felix said as he checked in with the executive team. "It feels very different in here. How have things been since our last session?"

"We're definitely making progress," Paul commented.

"We get along a lot better." Cedric seemed much more confident and relaxed.

"It's still not perfect," Iris said, "but Toby's been great. He's been helping us to learn to self manage and take responsibility for actions."

"And for our reactions and the impact we're having on each other," Kate added. "We're aware that there are various ripples in the organisation, but we understand that we're at a big edge for the whole company as we try to shift the culture and create a clear identity. We're getting some people on board. We're all paying attention to how we create reactions in people, and we're doing our best to avoid creating threats."

"How are you doing that?" Felix enquired.

"Well," Kate considered, "we allow people a certain amount of autonomy. We set a lot of context for why changes are coming, so as to create certainty and to allow people to feel in control. We've been assuring them that no one is going to lose their job. We all know it will take some time. And we recognise that some of them might not want to work for a company that is becoming a little less entrepreneurial, especially in the applications department."

"Good work," Felix nodded appreciatively. "Today, we're going to look at roles – in your teams and in the organisation. As you discovered with Leanne, there are external roles, for example, Sales, and there are internal roles."

"Like my whip-snapping," Frank surprised them all by getting in there first.

"We've all thought about it since the first session, and we know we do actually need Frank's whip, but without the snap," Paul agreed. "We had agreed back then that we'd share the responsibility."

"It sounds like you've done a lot of work together," Felix acknowledged. "What else might help with keeping up the team spirit?"

"Cedric gets on really well with most people," Iris pointed out. "He really knows how to get people to do their best."

"And Iris is great at getting teams to work together," Paul added. "Perhaps Cedric and Iris can help with keeping the team spirit up, keeping us all motivated."

Iris looked across at Cedric and stuck both her thumbs up in the air. "You and me, partner. We'll keep this mob in line."

"And if you can't, my whip will be waiting behind my door ..." Frank reminded them, a half-smile hovering on his lips. They all laughed.

"Iris and I can point out when reactions are flying around the table, too," Cedric volunteered. "If you all agree."

There was a general nodding and murmuring of agreement all round.

"It's not just about performance, though, is it?" Kate said. "We need to keep our vision of Sekhmed alive."

"That's why we're all here," George agreed.

"Exactly," she replied. "And you hold a really important role about the essence of Sekhmed."

"We need to hear more from you, George," Iris said.

"And we need to balance the inspiration of the original spirit of Sekhmed and the way we worked at that time," George said. "I know they're different things."

Team Coaching Session Four – Collaboration and Innovation

"We looked at the past and the present in the first three team coaching sessions," Felix said after the greetings and banter had stopped. "For our last session together, I invite you to have an innovation session about something you need to decide on. Is there anything that would be challenging for you to agree on?"

"Well," Paul stepped in, "now that you mention it – "

"We've been looking for ideas on how to make a great selling point," Iris cut in.

"But every time the subject comes up, we've ignored the *problem*," Paul finished, emphasising the last word with a grimace.

"Sounds perfect," Felix responded. "Who wants to kick off the discussion?"

They started with some safe options.

"Notice how you're all playing safe with these suggestions," Felix observed. "How about stretching yourselves a little? Formulate a question that you want a new answer to."

"How about, *How can we sell the idea to our customers that they can help with QA?*" Cedric suggested.

"Nice one, Cedric," George laughed. "Get the customer to do your job for you!"

Felix smiled. "You won't be surprised, by now, to hear that we're going to do things a little differently. We have different brain waves depending on the type of activity our brains are involved in," he explained. "When we're focussing hard on a problem, our brain is in its regular problem-solving mode. Usually at this stage, only typical solutions will be offered, solutions from the known. If we *really* want to be creative, we have to stretch into the unknown, where the limbic system might be a bit uncomfortable. First we give the PFC a break and allow the brain to get into a different mode – literally a different frequency – so that it can create new ideas."

He explained to the team that they would be listening to soft music for fifteen minutes, and then he would ask them to dream.

"Great, we get paid to sleep on the job!" Frank quipped. "Things are looking up."

They listened to the music. It was a little weird, Kate thought, but the energy in the room definitely shifted.

"Now write down any new, weird ... even strange ideas that come to you," Felix requested, "and then return to dream land."

After he turned off the music and they'd had a couple of minutes to write down further thoughts, Felix invited them to share their ideas.

It wasn't long before the eye-rolls and guffaws started. "Listen guys," Felix jumped in immediately. "Anything that sounds like personal criticism shuts down this process of creating something."

"I remember when Leanne was talking about creativity during the training session," George said, "and we realised you're not going to risk putting new ideas out if you're not feeling safe."

"Exactly so," Felix agreed. "And you won't be very creative if you're busy focussing either. That's the whole point of this process."

"We listen to music and drift off into a dream state so that our brains stop focussing," Paul mused.

"Once we've got a whole bunch of ideas, the next step is to get critical," Felix told them, "so we need to think about what will help you to feel safe."

They spent a few minutes making agreements that they wouldn't take criticism of an idea personally, and they wouldn't criticise individuals for their ideas, even if they criticised the idea itself.

They learned to build, shape and re-shape ideas.

"This is actually quite fun!" Iris commented. "Our customers are going to love helping us with our new QA process!"

"I don't believe it," Kate said at the end of the day. "We've actually discussed a *problem*, all of us, without checking out or killing each other. I'm impressed with us."

Notes from Chapter 17

- Individual coaching happens between team coaching sessions, and each of the executive team members work at varying paces on their own personal development, such as learning to manage their own reactions towards the others.

- The individual work is about self-awareness, self-management and self-responsibility.

- Team coaching one: The team works together on noticing their impact on each other and working together as a team with fewer limbic reactions, drama triangles and toxic behviour patterns.

- Team coaching two: the team works together on their identity and edges they need to cross. They also look at how individualistic they are.

- Team coaching three: The team works through their various roles – both inner and outer roles.

- Team coaching four: The team realises they have learned how to collaborate by managing all those reactions and drama. They move to implementing some simple innovation techniques and realise it is much easier to be creative when their brains are not focused on fear.

18. Phase Four - Rollout and On-Going Support

The executive team was in good shape. They knew much more about how to work together and where their trouble spots were. They had learned to collaborate. A key element had been learning to have productive conflicts and to work through issues before they turned into deep-seated revenge and resentment. They had learned to see the roles that were needed in order to be a fully-functioning system; sometimes they would have to shift roles, eliminate roles, or create new roles, whether those were internal or external roles. They had definitely learned how to speak to each other in ways that were less toxic and reactive and to keep positivity alive on their team.

They had also learned that a more collaborative team created the foundation for finding new and innovative solutions to the problems they faced. And they learned to use their brains in a different way when creativity and innovation were called for.

Each of them had grown in the process – they had to in order for the whole team to grow and change. And now they realised that there was work to do with the rest of the company as well.

Rollout

In collaboration with Kate, the coaches created a plan for training the rest of Sekhmed. The management team wanted to make sure that all Sekhmed employees had the opportunity to learn about the brain and self-management techniques. And they wanted to make sure that everyone knew what the leaders were now practising and implementing in their daily work. They knew this was critical if the leaders were going to be successful in working differently with their teams.

The coaches created a shortened version of the leadership development programme. The content was oriented towards communication and collaboration skills and could be applied in all of their teams and departments. Staff learned about limbic reactions and recovery techniques, edges and edge behaviour, drama triangles and other dynamics that show up in everyday work situations. They learned to address and manage conflict. As expected, some employees embraced the ideas wholeheartedly and some resisted, but at least they knew what was happening in Sekhmed. Many found that learning about brain-friendly working was much easier to understand and accept than "soft skills" they had heard about in the past.

Felix facilitated some specific team coaching sessions where there were hotspots – specifically Maintenance together with Cedric and between Sales and the software developers.

On-Going Support

Sekhmed management had already learned that change takes time. New behaviours and skills needed to be reinforced and practised. Real change would take place as people used these new skills together in their teams and working groups.

Management made sure that support was provided for both individuals and systems. Toby, as an external coach, was on contract to support individuals in their growth and change processes. Both Felix and Leanne were available to support team challenges.

Sekhmed also invested in training a couple of the staff members who were interested in learning to coach individuals. Two of the team leaders learned more about systems coaching and resolving conflicts. They became the internal resources for team facilitation.

In addition to building internal resources, Felix was occasionally invited to come in and help a new project team get started in a positive direction. At other times, he would sit in on meetings and help the team notice where they got themselves into reactive territory or potential conflict. He provided tips – mostly reminders – on how to run more brain-friendly meetings and team interactions.

There was now recognition across the company that conflict happens: we are human beings and we disagree sometimes. Most of the teams took time to create agreements and started paying attention to their working relationships. They addressed conflicts more openly and started seeking help from their Sekhmed colleagues who had been trained in conflict management, or they called in one of the external coaches when their conflicts were more difficult to address.

The executive team committed to receiving regular reminders and tips from Felix and Leanne and wholeheartedly agreed to have short refresher sessions with them every six months.

Sekhmed's Results

At the end of the year, the executive team reviewed their current situation and the changes they had made. The Sales team had begun to talk to the developers more, and they felt more empowered to say no to some customer requests. They reduced the number of special applications in sales contracts. As a result, Sekhmed's revenue had dropped but profits increased.

One of the hotshot developers who had previously encouraged a lot of the specialised apps decided that he didn't like the direction of Sekhmed's working environment, so he resigned and looked for a faster-paced company to work with. They were sorry to lose him, but most recognised that was the best for everyone.

Informal conversations throughout the year made it clear that customers were feeling more valued and happier with Sekhmed's service. Several customers got involved with the QA analysis and implementation, and there too, they felt valued and listened to.

The management team was confident that they were absolutely on the right track. Their new customer service reviews were due any day, and they had no doubt they would be vastly improved over previous years.

The Corporation had also seen that things were changing at Sekhmed. They praised Kate highly for the work she did with her division. While one part of her wanted to take all the credit, she really knew the credit belonged to the management team and the employees.

Notes from Chapter 18

- A one-day programme similar to the leadership programme is rolled out to the rest of the organisation, so all can benefit from information about the brain and how to manage reactions.

- A plan for maintenance is put in place to create reminders for everyone – on the individual and executive team level.

PART 6
What's Next?

19. Change Does Not Come Naturally

A lot of people know that change in organisations is very difficult to implement and that it rarely truly succeeds. There's good reason for these many failures because there are so many forces working against successful change.

On the individual level, we have our limbic systems that are paranoid about any changes: we like stability, certainty and predictability. Without those, the limbic system reacts and creates fear responses: we run, we freeze and we fight.

Our PFCs are inherently lazy. To do something new and different, we have to focus our attention on how to do the new thing, which takes expensive brain power. It's so much easier to rely on our Basal Ganglia to guide us in doing what we've always done.

We have individual habits. We have learned to be successful in the way we currently do things. Having to change that means we have to get uncomfortable. We have to give up some of the dopamine boosts we get every time we are successful if we are to let go of that success. Then we might fail in the new thing, and that's really hard.

On the systemic level, we have a culture that tells us who we are. It helps us to know how we belong and to whom we belong. If we change that, we change our relationship to the whole. Reactions happen.

Reactions give rise to other reactions. People tend to band together around an identity. If there are a number of people who want to resist change, they are likely to form a tribe against what the organisation is "doing to them."

So Should We Just Give Up?

No, we don't think so. But we do need to have our eyes open and be aware that resistance will happen. We can anticipate it and perhaps prevent a lot of it. We can create a different type of reward.

Realise that change takes time. You are in for a marathon, not a sprint.

Companies can encourage the personal development required for people to be able to self-manage and take personal responsibility for their individual actions. They can also encourage training about limbic systems and recovery techniques.

Leaders need to make sure everyone has some choice in how they implement their change. They also need to ensure there's something people can align with in those changes, something that will address the questions: *Who will we be then? What's in it for me?*

Above all, safety needs to be created. The brain will readily go to "What's in it for me?" or perhaps, more honestly: "Will I lose my job, my status?"

People need to be trained and developed in context. It helps for them to have gatherings such as courses, team coaching and meetings where safety is created, and where they feel safe enough to talk about what they need during the change.

It is important to understand enough of the neuroscience and the systems thinking for leaders and their people to have a vocabulary to talk about what's going on during the change. It is very helpful if we understand that these reactions and behaviours are "natural," and not done because people want to be "difficult."

The main emphasis for Maintenance is that there actually *is* some: practise the tools. Create agreements about who will be in charge of setting up team agreements and who will help the team stay clean about communication styles.

Most organisations have a version of saying: "Our people are our most valuable asset." Make it real. Make the focus on people a part of your leaders' KPIs, and create a culture where people get to be honest and unafraid.

Encourage collectivism. Create a culture that people want to belong to and that they're proud of. Give them a reason to reduce their individual focus and "lean in" to the collective. This isn't to say that organisations should become cults where people lose their individual identity. (Please no!) We can find a balance where the collective is interesting and powerful but not all-consuming and harmful.

It is possible to change the culture of an organisation to a more humane one: a culture where people bring all of themselves to work; a culture where they collaborate within conscious and intentional agreements; a culture where they are allowed to be innovative, and where the results are beneficial to both the organisation and to the people within them.

Tips

Recognise everyone for the great job they're already doing. No matter what that is, find something that they're doing well. It's likely they were trying to do something beneficial. Try to find the good intention behind their actions. Maybe it was a little self-focussed, and they need to be nudged towards a team focus. Make that interesting or even exciting for them. Help them to want to belong. Go for creating belonging boosts, even if they might get a status hit.

Create an inspiring vision that people will want to belong to and align with.

Pay attention to relationship and make time for it. Teams with great relationships work better together and are much more efficient, creative, innovative...

Structures

Have brain-friendly meetings. Create certainty and clarity.

When an organisation is undergoing a change process, it is often useful to make some other changes as well – perhaps some physical changes. While this is more for the PFC to handle, it will disrupt some of the well-connected associations. For example, if people sit in different chairs at meetings, some of the old communication patterns might be changed more easily.

Allow people to choose where they work. Perhaps allow people to work from home or choose their working hours.

Create a way for conflicts to be aired.

Notes from Chapter 19

- Change is difficult; the brain doesn't like it.

- Change takes time as there are habits to break and habits to learn.

- Encourage personal development. Personal development is not scary or weird, it is practical and necessary for any larger change to happen.

- Create ways to practise new tools, and allow space and time for imperfection and learning.

- Encourage collectivism, but it will only happen if the individual feels safe and secure.

- Let's learn to use our brains together.

Conclusion

There is a lot of suffering in organisations and for the people who work in them. It's as if the company has forgotten that there are human beings serving it and the employees have forgotten that they are part of something larger than themselves. If something is going to change, we need to address both sides. Sure, we want people to be more company-minded, but is the company going to be more people-minded? They must happen together.

The problems in organisations are often complex and entangled. We need to get to the bottom of them rather than try to fix the symptoms. At the bottom, we will probably find limbic system reactions. Perhaps the owners of the company are trying to squeeze more out of the employees, so the company can compete better in the marketplace. Perhaps the employees are just trying to protect themselves from abuse from their boss – who's only trying to do his job.

We strive for more, more, more because our limbic systems tell us we have to do so in order to survive. We're pushed so far and so fast that we're scrambling and reacting without really thinking. We're in survival mode, and we don't take the time to think or to be in relationship. There aren't any sabre tooth tigers out to get us, but we behave as if there are.

We have a beautiful resource in our brains, and we can learn to use it. If we do that together, if we team up and use our great brain resources together, we can make some significant changes.

Our brains are incredible instruments. Let's learn to use them, together. When we collaborate – truly collaborate from a place of feeling safe, where we don't worry about survival – we can create high functioning, nurturing, creative, innovative teams that produce great results. Together.

Together. It takes all of us to Team Up and make changes together.

References

Introduction

Lessons from Neuroscience

Lesson: the brain creates habits and relies on habits to function every day.

Ashby FG, Turner BO, Horvitz JC. "Cortical and Basal Ganglia Contributions to Habit Learning and Automaticity". *Trends in Cognitive Sciences,* 2010

Wise, Stephen P. "The Role of the Basal Ganglia in Procedural Memory." *Seminars in Neuroscience,* 1996.

Lesson: our brains are not hardwired – we can learn to do things differently.

Schwartz, Jeffrey and Begley, Sharon. *The Mind and the Brain: Neuroplasticity and the Power of Mental Force.* Harper Perennial, 2004

Lesson: The brain's focus on survival drives us to be protective of our needs and fearful of perceived threats.

Gordon, Evian. *Integrative Neuroscience: Bringing Together Biological, Psychological and Clinical Models of the Human Brain.* CRC Press, 2000.

Lesson: The brain is a social brain, designed to be in relationship with others.

Cozolino, Louis. *The Neuroscience of Human Relationships: Attachment and the Developing Social Brain (2nd edition) (Norton Series on Interpersonal Neurobiology).* W. W. Norton & Company, 2014

Goleman, Daniel. *Social Intelligence: The Revolutionary New Science of Human Relationships.* Bantam Books, 2006.

Lesson: The brain is extremely good at filling in the gaps, i.e. making assumptions.

Hsu M, Bhatt M, Adolphs R, Tranel D, Camerer CF. "Neural Systems Responding to Degrees of Uncertainty in Human Decision-Making." *Science,* 2005

Clark, Andy. "Whatever next? Predictive Brains, Situated Agents, and the Future of Cognitive Science." *School of Philosophy, Psychology, and Language Sciences, University of Edinburgh, Scotland, UK,* 2013

Schultz, Wolfram. "The Reward Signal of Midbrain Dopamine Neurons." *Physiology,* 1999

PART 2 Neuroscience

The drive for survival

Gordon, Evian. *Integrative Neuroscience: Bringing Together Biological, Psychological and Clinical Models of the Human Brain.* CRC Press, 2000.

Cozolino, Louis. *The Neuroscience of Human Relationships: Attachment and the Developing Social Brain (2nd edition) (Norton Series on Interpersonal Neurobiology).* W. W. Norton & Company, 2014

Belonging

Naomi I. Eisenberger NI, Lieberman ND, and Williams KD. "Does Rejection Hurt? An fMRI Study of Social Exclusion." *Science,* 2003

Status

Zink CF, Tong Y, Chen Q, Bassett DS, Stein JL, Meyer-Lindenberg A. "Know Your Place: Neural Processing of Social Hierarchy in Humans." *Neuron,* 2008.

Izuma K, Saito DN, Sadato N. "Processing of Social and Monetary Rewards in the Human Striatum." *Neuron,* 2008

Fairness

Singer T, Seymour B, O'Doherty JP, Stephan KE, Dolan RJ, Frith CD. "Empathic neural responses are modulated by the perceived fairness of others." *Nature*, 2006

Certainty

Schultz, Wolfram. "The Reward Signal of Midbrain Dopamine Neurons." *Physiology*, 1999

Autonomy

Mineka S, Hendersen RW. "Controllability and Predictability in Acquired motivation." *Annual Review of Psychology*, 1985

Empathy

Rameson LT, Lieberman MD. "Empathy: A Social Cognitive Neuroscience Approach." *Social and Personality Psychology Compass,* 2009

Keysers, Christian. *The Empathic Brain: How the Discovery of Mirror Neurons Change our Understanding of Human Nature.* Social Brain Press, 2011

Error detection

Carter CS, Braver TS, Barch DM, Botvinick MM, Noll D, Cohen JD. "Anterior Cingulate Cortex, Error Detection, and the Online Monitoring of Perfromance." *Science,* 1998

The human benefit – the prefrontal cortex

Dispenza, Joe. *Evolve Your Brain: The Science of Changing Your Mind.* Health Communications, 2009

Goleman, Daniel. *Emotional Intelligence: Why It Can Matter More Than IQ.* Bloomsbury Publishing, 2009

Consciously focused attention and the limited PFC

Siegal, Daniel J. *The Mindful Brain: Reflection and Attunement in the Cultivation of Well-Being (Norton Series on Interpersonal Neurobiology).* W. W. Norton & Company, 2007

Schwartz, Jeffrey and Begley, Sharon. *The Mind and the Brain: Neuroplasticity and the Power of Mental Force.* Harper Perennial, 2004

Rock, David and Schwartz, Jeffrey. "The Neuroscience of Leadership" *Strategy+Business* Issue 43

Focus on people

Hogeveen J, Inzlicht M, Obhi SS. "Power Changes How the Brain Responds to Others.*" Journal of Experimental Psychology: General,* 2013

Efficiency and the habit-making machine

Ashby FG, Turner BO, Horvitz JC. "Cortical and Basal Ganglia Contributions to Habit Learning and Automaticity". *Trends in Cognitive Sciences,* 2010

Begley, Sharon. *Train Your Mind, Change Your Brain: How a New Science Reveals Our Extraordinary Potential to Transform Ourselves.* Ballantine Books; Reprint edition, 2008

Packard MG, Knowlton BJ. "Learning and Memory Functions of the Basal Ganglia." *Annual Review of Neuroscience,* 2002

PART 3 Systems Thinking

Introduction to our social brains

Cozolino, Louis. *The Neuroscience of Human Relationships: Attachment and the Developing Social Brain (2ⁿᵈ edition) (Norton Series on Interpersonal Neurobiology).* W. W. Norton & Company, 2014

Goleman, Daniel. Social Intelligence: *The Revolutionary New Science of Human Relationships.* Bantam Books, 2006.

Lieberman, Daniel. *Social: Why Our Brains Are Wired to Connect.* Crown, 2013

Also see Family Systems Theory by Dr. Murray Bowen, available in many forms and locations on the internet.

Cummins, Denise Delarose. "The Evolution of Reasoning." *The Nature of Reasoning edited by Jacqueline P. Leighton and Robert J. Sternberg.* The Press Syndicate of the University of Cambridge, 2004

Humans exist in tribes

Tooby J, Cosmides L. "The Psychological Foundations of Culture." *The Adapted Mind: Evolutionary Psychology and the Generation of Culture edited by Jerome H. Barkow et al.* Oxford University Press, 1992

Individualism versus collectivism

Decety J, Jackson PL, Sommerville JA, Chaminade T, Meltzoff AN. "The neural bases of cooperation and competition: an fMRI investigation." *NeuroImage,* 2004

Hofstede, Geert; Hofstede, Gert Jan and Minkov, Michael. *Cultures and Organizations: Software of the Mind, Third Edition.* McGraw-Hill, 2010

Individual Leadership

Binney, George; Williams, Collins and Wilke, Gerhard. *Living Leadership: A Practical Guide for Ordinary Heroes.* Financial Time/ Prentice Hall; 2nd edition, 2009

Edge Model

See Organisation and Relationship Systems Coaching curriculum offered by CRRGlobal.

PART 4 Using What We Know.

Chapter 10. Leadership Development

Recovery

Tabibnia G, Monterosso JR, Baicy K, Aron AR, Poldrack RA, Chakrapani S, Lee B, London ED. "Different Forms of Self-Control Share a Neurocognitive Substrate." *Journal of Neuroscience,* 2014

Lieberman MD, Eisenberger NI, Crockett MJ, Tom SM, Pfeifer JH, Way BM. "Putting Feelings Into Words: Affect Labeling Disrupts

Amygdala Activity in Response to Affective Stimuli." *Psychological Science,* 2007

Creswell JD, Way BM, Eisenberger NI and Lieberman MD. "Neural Correlates of Dispositional Mindfulness During Affect Labeling." *Psychological Science,* 2007

Positivity

Bono J, Glomb T, Shen W, Kim E, Koch A. "Building Positive Resources: Effects of Positive Events and Positive Reflection on Work Stress and Health." *Academy of Management Journal,* 2013

Oswald AJ, Proto E, and Sgroi D. "Happiness and Productivity" *JOLE,* 2014

Some systems dynamics

Gottman, John. *The Seven Principles for Making Marriage Work.* Crown Archetype, 2002

The drama triangle is a psychological and social model of human interaction in transactional analysis (TA) first described by Stephen Karpman, in his 1968 article "Fairy Tales and Script Drama Analysis"

Chapter 11. Experiential Training and Coaching

Davachi L, Kiefer T, Rock D and Rock L. "Learning that lasts through AGES." *NeuroLeadership Journal,* 2010

Semantic memory

Jacoby LL, Dallas M. "Semantic Memory: On the relationship between autobiographical memory and perceptual learning." *Journal of Experimental Psychology: General,* 1981

Episodic memory

Davachi L, Wagner AD. "Hippocampal Contributions to Episodic Encoding: Insights from Relational and Item-Based Learning." *Journal of Neurophysiology,* 2002

Davachi L, Dobbins IG. "Declarative Memory." *Current Directions in Psychological Science,* 2008

Procedural memory

Wise, Stephen P. "The Role of the Basal Ganglia in Procedural Memory." *Seminars in Neuroscience,* 1996

Natural Learning

György G, Gergely C. "The social construction of the cultural mind: Imitative learning as a mechanism of human pedagogy" *Interaction Studies*, John Benjamins Publishing Company, 2005

Zull, James E. *From Brain to Mind: The Developmental Journey from Mimicry to Creative Thought Through Experience and Education.* Stylus Publishing, 2011

Pointing attention

Hedden T, Gabrieli JDE. "The Ebb and Flow of Attention in the Human Brain." *Nature Neuroscience,* 2006

Set up for success

Kensinger EA, Clarke RJ, Corkin S. "What Neural Correlates Underlie Successful Encoding and Retrieval? A Functional Magnetic Resonance Imaging Study Using a Divided Attention Paradigm." *The Journal of Neuroscience,* 2003

Other Books and References

Lencioni, Patrick M. *The Five Dysfunctions of a Team: A Leadership Fable.* Jossey-Bass, 2011

Rock, David. *Your Brain at Work, Strategies for Overcoming Distraction, Regaining Focus & Working Smarter All Day Long.* Harper Business, 2009

Siegal, Daniel J. *Mindsight: The New Science of Personal Transformation.* Bantam, 2010

Whitworth, Laura; Kimsey-House, Henry; Kimsey-House Karen and Sandahl, Philip. *Co-Active Coaching, 3rd Edition: Changing Business, Transforming Lives.* Nicholas Brealey Publishing, 2011

Other Places for More Information

The Journal of Social Neuroscience

The NeuroLeadership Institute

CRRGlobal

Printed in Great Britain
by Amazon